DUKE · UNIVERSITY · PUBLICATIONS

SHAKESPEARE

and the

Popular Dramatic Tradition

Photograph by G. E. Ho

CROSS SECTION OF AN ELIZABETHAN THEATER

The model is constructed to scale (½ inch:1 foot), and the proportions are based on the specifications for the Fortune Theatre, for which the builder's contract survives. Certain features of the Globe and the Swan are incorporated. The main features, however, were common to all Elizabethan "public" theaters (excepting that there was, perhaps, no "inner stage" at the Swan). The model, which is in the custody of the English Department of University College, Cardiff, has been photographed and reproduced by the kind permission of the owner, who designed and constructed it—Miss L. M. R. Cattley (B.A., Oxon.).

SHAKESPEARE

and the

Popular Dramatic Tradition

By S. L. BETHELL, M.A., Cantab.

INTRODUCTION BY T. S. ELIOT

1970

OCTAGON BOOKS

New York

Reprinted 1970
by special arrangement with Duke University Press

OCTAGON BOOKS
A Division of Farrar, Straus & Giroux, Inc.
19 Union Square West
New York, N. Y. 10003

Library of Congress Catalog Card Number: 75-120230

To my revered and beloved Father,

OLIVER BETHELL

who died on the first of January, 1938,

I dedicate this book,

in gratitude for his example of Christian life, and for the patient criticism and encouragement to which I owe in great measure whatever may be of value in my work. May God grant him perpetual light and peace.

INTRODUCTION

As THE VOLUME of Shakespeare criticism increases, year by year, the common reader must be inclined to wonder, what has all this to do with him? and to reiterate the objection, that what really matters is the plays themselves, and not what an endless succession of critics say about them. The science of textual criticism he admits, and pays a remote respect to the scholar who removes or inserts a comma; the discovery of another biographical fact is at least a sensation; and the structure of the Tudor and Jacobean stage is a question of legitimate archaeological curiosity. But of all these matters of investigation the common reader believes there must some day be an end: the prospect that the questions will be finally answered is the justification for asking them. But of interpretative criticism, which is the relating of historical fact to contemporary consciousness, there is no end; so the reader is tempted to ask, to what purpose is a journey without a terminus?

The answer to *this* question would itself have to take the form of a book—which itself would have to be succeeded, in a generation or two, by another book—on the history of Shakespeare criticism, exhibiting that criticism as a history, in one aspect, of the English and the European mind. We all know that Shakespeare has presented a different appearance to every age. In the work of any Shakespeare critic of the past we can see, when we have made the deduction of individual genius and individual limitations, the outlines of the consciousness of the critic's age. It is possible that one age may miss what a previous age had grasped. There are variations also, under the influence of a passing philosophy. One age may see

Shakespeare more in the study, another more in the theater. At a particular moment, and sometimes in a particular place, certain of the less popular plays may have a particular appeal: we remember the limited, but significant interest in *Troilus and Cressida* a few years ago. But on the whole, we must assume (as posterity will assume after us) that we are in a better position to understand Shakespeare than any of our predecessors. This is not merely an assumption of the Shakespeare critic, or of the literary critic in general, but the assumption implicit in all historical study: that we understand the past better than previous generations did, simply because there is more of it. We assume, and must assume, a progressive development of consciousness.

The constant reader of Shakespeare should be also, to the best of his opportunities, the constant theatergoer: for any play of Shakespeare requires to be seen and heard, as well as read, many times; and seen and heard in as many different productions as possible. But however much he frequents the theater, he probably does not realize the extent to which stage production has been influenced by criticism. (His best approach might be the other way about, studying the *Prefaces* of Harley Granville-Barker for the contribution of a dramatist and producer to criticism.) This influence is not necessarily quite direct; but it is possible that some future producer who has read this book by Mr. Bethell, will present a *Hamlet* rather different, in consequence, from previous *Hamlets*. Meanwhile, however, the reader may ask himself, why need I be conscious of all these things in Shakespeare's plays, of which Shakespeare himeslf was perhaps not quite conscious? Why can I not enjoy the play simply, as a contemporary would have done? The answer is, of course, that we cannot escape from the criticism of the past except through the criticism of the present.

The extent to which the past weighs upon us, and forces upon our attention problems which for the contemporary did not exist, has been brought home to me in attempting to cope with the difficulties of writing verse drama today. It is only a humble statement of fact, to say that the verse dramatist today has to be much more conscious of what he is doing than Shakespeare was, and, even to produce a result comparatively trifling, has to surmount obstacles which to Shakespeare were unknown. For instance, a poet, trying to write something for the theater, discovers first of all that it is not only a question of laboring to acquire the technique of the theater: it is a question of a different kind of poetry, a different kind of verse, than the kind for which his previous experience has qualified him. How, he must ask himself, would people today speak if they could speak in poetry? They cannot be translated to a fairyland where they may talk appropriately in verse; they must on your stage be able to perform the same actions, and lead the same lives, as in the real world. But they must somehow disclose (not necessarily be aware of) a deeper reality than that of the plane of most of our conscious living; and what they disclose must be, not the psychologist's intellectualization of this reality, but the reality itself. And the poetry must express, in a way in which natural speech cannot, not only the reality of the individual, but the reality of a situation composed of a fusion, in sympathy or antipathy, of two or more individuals. A verse play is not a play done into verse, but a different kind of play: in a way more realistic than "naturalistic drama," because, instead of clothing nature in poetry, it should remove the surface of things, expose the underneath, or the inside, of the natural surface appearance. It may allow the characters to behave inconsistently, but only with respect to a deeper consistency. It may use any device to show their real feelings and volitions, instead of just what, in actual life, they would normally profess or be conscious of; it must reveal, underneath the vacillating or infirm character, the indomitable unconscious will; and underneath the resolute purpose of the planning animal, the victim of circumstance and the doomed or sanctified being. So the poet with ambitions of the theater, must discover the laws, both of another kind of verse and of another kind of drama. The difficulty of the author is also the difficulty of the audience. Both have to be trained; both need to be conscious of many things which neither an Elizabethan dramatist, nor an Elizabethan audience, had any need to know; and if a book like Mr. Bethell's is helpful to the writer of verse plays, I am sure that it should be to those who hear and read them also.

T. S. ELIOT.

February 19, 1944.

ACKNOWLEDGMENTS

EVERY WRITER upon Shakespeare must owe a great deal to his predecessors and contemporaries in the field. I am aware of the deepest obligation to the general critical writings of Mr. T. S. Eliot and Dr. F. R. Leavis, but I am indebted especially and specifically to the Shakespearean criticism of Professor Schücking, Dr. E. M. W. Tillyard, Miss M. C. Bradbrook, and Dr. L. C. Knights; also to Professor Wilson Knight's interesting volume, *The Wheel of Fire*. I have tried to indicate in footnotes the sources of ideas not my own, but there must be a great many that I have failed to acknowledge, and for which I hope this general acknowledgment may suffice. Not infrequently I am compelled to disagree with those to whom my debt is greatest. I have criticized the critics somewhat closely, and tried to show precisely where I agree or disagree with them. It seems to me a deplorable tendency in modern criticism to bring out books which entirely ignore the work of other writers on the same subject. For criticism is a co-operative function which thrives on controversy. The sharpest disagreement may be in the nature of a compliment: only a bland ignoring of the other person's point of view should bear the stigma of critical bad manners.

I am grateful to my colleague, the Reverend W. M. Merchant, for criticism and advice, and to my old friend, Mr. A. N. Lancaster, for carefully preparing my manuscript, at some inconvenience to himself, in a London cellar during the German air raids. My debt to Mr. Eliot, a large one already, has been greatly increased by his courtesy in writing the Introduction. My wife's help has, as always, been invaluable.

Several publishers have kindly allowed me to quote from copyright works: full references to these will be found in the footnotes.

S. L. B.

Cardiff.

Note to the American Edition

It is deeply gratifying that in the midst of all the burdens of war, my colleagues in the American academic world have taken upon themselves the labor and trouble of presenting an edition of this book to the great American public concerned for the study of our joint literary heritage. British and Americans are now working together in the prosecution of war, but for many years we have been co-operating in the deep and permanent matters of peace and civilization. American criticism has won for itself a high place in the esteem of English men of letters, and I am glad to be received among Americans as an ally in the cause of humane culture. Shakespeare is not only the greatest poet and dramatist in our language, but his works provide the most profound expression of our religious and social tradition. The interpretation and reinterpretation of Shakespeare thus becomes the permanent duty of English-speaking people in war and peace.

I must thank very warmly the authorities of Duke University and its Press for their extreme kindness and patience in producing my book under the greatest difficulties. Communication between us has been slow and uncertain, and the reader is asked to pardon any imperfections which may arise from that circumstance. I cannot conclude without expressing the utmost obligation to my friend (as I hope I may call him, though we have never met in the flesh), Professor G. R. Elliott, of Amherst College, Massachusetts, who took charge of my manuscript and carried on all the irksome correspondence connected with it, despite a great press of wartime duties. Without his indefatigable good nature this edition could never have appeared. His unvaried courtesy has borne eloquent testimony to the reality of Anglo-American friendship in the academic sphere.   S. L. B.

CONTENTS

SHAKESPEARE

and the

Popular Dramatic Tradition

CHAPTER I

CONVENTIONALISM AND NATURALISM

FROM time to time and from place to place the drama varies its position on a scale between the two extremes of absolute conventionalism and absolute naturalism. At either extreme it would cease to be properly dramatic. Absolute conventionalism would work in symbols bearing no necessary relation to the things symbolized, and absolute naturalism would reproduce a "slice of life" with more than photographic fidelity. The former would be devoid of emotive power, like the symbols in algebra, whilst the latter would lack both intellectual and emotional organization. Actually the drama is never completely arbitrary in symbolism or completely and unselectively representational, although the difference, for example, between *Everyman* and *A Doll's House* is sufficient for the terms "conventional" and "naturalistic" to be applied to them respectively. *Everyman* represents allegorically the soul's conflict in its journey through life, and most of its characters personify abstract human qualities: Good Deeds, Knowledge, Strength, Discretion; but in *A Doll's House* everyday people are presented in everyday surroundings, the dialogue is conversational, and the action such as might take place in a contemporary household.

The position of Shakespeare is somewhere between these two practical extremes. His characters are not merely personified abstractions, but, on the other hand, they are not precisely like real people: for instance, they usually speak in verse. Conventionalism of this kind is so obvious, however, that nineteenth-century critics seem not to have reflected upon its implications; it was usual for them to treat Shakespeare as Ibsen is more appropriately treated: they fastened upon his characters as if they were historical personages, examining their psychology, weighing motives, allotting praise or blame to individual speeches and actions—even attempting to explain problems of character by imaginatively constructing the early life of Hamlet or Othello. There was no attempt to consider the historical anomaly by which a naturalistic drama could so quickly have arisen out of a conventional tradition. Behind the Elizabethan drama were generations of miracle plays and interludes, including "moralities" such as *Everyman*; they had not quite disappeared in the boyhood of Shakespeare himself. More recent investigation has accorded them their proper place as forerunners of the Elizabethan drama, which has been shown to have more in common with its conventional ancestry than used to be suspected.

Attention directed to the physical conditions of the Elizabethan theater has revealed a number of conventions in dramatic production which are plainly survivals of the long-continued popular tradition of conventional drama. In *Romeo and Juliet,* to choose a popular example,[1] we are presented in Act I, scene iv, with a party of maskers on their way to the Capulets' feast. At the end of the scene, according to a contemporary stage direction, "they march about the stage";[2] and in the next scene, after a brief passage of comedy, Capulet delivers his speech of welcome to the guests and maskers. The maskers have thus, without leaving the stage, translated them-

---

[1] Cf. C. M. Haines, "The Development of Shakespeare's Stagecraft," in *Shakespeare and the Theatre*, by Members of the Shakespeare Association (London: Oxford University Press, 1927), p. 43.

[2] The Globe edition has been used for all Shakespearean references and quotations, except when, as here, there is some other indication in the text.

selves from a street to a hall in the Capulets' house, by
this conventional "marching about," accompanied presumably by a conventional disclosure of the much disputed
"inner stage." Now the miracle plays were often presented
on a "multiple" stage, on which more than one locality
was represented at the same time, and "journeys" might
be undertaken from one such locality to another: Our
Lord might thus be shown journeying between the judgment halls of Herod and Pilate, which would be represented by structures on different parts of the stage. The
maskers' "marching about" would seem to be a survival
of such conventional "journeying." The suggestion[3] that
they walk round the back of the stage—"off" and "on"
again—seems a much less likely interpretation of the
stage direction. *Richard III*, Act V, scene iii, provides
another and less disputable instance of the survival of
multiple-stage technique. The stage represents Bosworth
Field on the eve of battle, with the tents of the rival
generals pitched at opposite sides—stage distance bearing
no more relation to real distance than on the multiple
stage. The ghosts, when they enter (presumably by a
trap door, center stage), are thus enabled to pronounce
maledictions upon Richard and blessings upon Richmond,
turning solemnly from one side of the stage to the other.
Miss Bradbrook suggests[4] that Richmond may have occupied the inner stage, but the principle is the same in
either event.

Psychological naturalism as the basis of Shakespearean
criticism, reached its limit in A. C. Bradley's *Shakespearean Tragedy*.[5] But already the physical conditions
of Shakespeare's theater had been patiently investigated;
and this new knowledge, coupled with the historical and

[3] Mentioned by Miss M. C. Bradbrook in *Elizabethan Stage Conditions*
(Cambridge University Press, 1932), pp. 38-39.
[4] *Ibid.*, p. 36.
[5] London: Macmillan & Co., 1904; 2d ed., 1905.

comparative study of Shakespeare and his predecessors and contemporaries, was to produce among daring spirits a violent reaction against the psychological approach. Professor Schücking's treatise, translated as *Character Problems in Shakespeare's Plays*,[6] shows how far even the presentation of character depends on stage convention rather than the direct representation of life. Apart from this seminal idea, however, the book is of doubtful value. Professor Schücking cannot appreciate the depth and subtlety of Shakespeare's verse, and though he claims Shakespeare as conventional rather than naturalistic, his sympathies seem to be with modern naturalism, so that he is also incapable of appreciating the dramatic subtleties made available by a conventional tradition. He speaks disparagingly of Shakespeare's "primitive" art-form and seems to confuse primitive technique with naïveté of thought and feeling. Believing in Shakespeare's naïveté, he misses all his deeper meaning, and endlessly multiplies conventions in order to account for everything he cannot understand. Professor Stoll, in his *Art and Artifice in Shakespeare*,[7] has pushed the argument of Professor Schücking even farther, since to him Shakespeare's every tragic hero is built upon a contradiction impossible to psychology but rendered plausible by dramatic and poetic art: Shakespeare's object is "emotional illusion."[8] However far we may feel Professors Schücking and Stoll to be from a profound and comprehensive view of Shakespeare, they have certainly revealed a body of dramatic conventions unsuspected by an earlier generation of critics. We are told that, on the Elizabethan stage, disguise was conventionally impenetrable, slander was conventionally believed, and characters conformed to type: the Avenger,

[6] London: George G. Harrap & Co., 1922.
[7] Cambridge University Press, 1933.
[8] *Ibid.*, p. 49.

the Machiavel, the Melancholy Man. The villain was conventionally—not cynically—aware of his own villainy, and the hero—without priggishness—of his own virtues. It is all useful knowledge, provided we remember that these are not rules but sweeping generalities, and certainly not true of every instance. We can be safe only in a close study of each individual text. The greatest contribution to Shakespearean criticism has not, in fact, come from the specialists, but from those general critics who have taught us to take his poetry seriously, and to realize that, in Shakespeare, poetry and drama are not separable ingredients, but that the drama is a poetic creation, existing in the poetry like a Thomist *universale in re*. The suggestions of Mr. T. S. Eliot[9] and Dr. F. R. Leavis[10] have been followed out by Miss Bradbrook[11] and Dr. L. C. Knights:[12] the time has gone by for anthologizing Shakespeare's "beauties," and the poetry has at last been accorded that fundamental position which it naturally holds. It is difficult to see how it can ever have been otherwise—how the poetry can ever have been treated as a decorative inessential. The immense superiority of *Antony and Cleopatra* over Dryden's *All for Love* is quite clearly a superiority in poetry. Indeed, strip the poetry from a play of Shakespeare, and what is left but a rather haphazard story about a set of vaguely outlined and incredibly "stagey" characters? There is no originality of plot, little subtlety of psychological analysis,

[9] They appeared first in *The Sacred Wood* (London: Methuen & Co., Ltd., 1920), but see *Selected Essays, 1917-1932* (London: Faber & Faber, 1932).

[10] See *How to Teach Reading, a Primer for Ezra Pound* (Cambridge, England: G. Fraser; The Minority Press, 1932).

[11] In *Elizabethan Stage Conditions*, and in *Themes and Conventions of Elizabethan Tragedy* (Cambridge University Press, 1935).

[12] *How Many Children Had Lady Macbeth?* (Cambridge, England: G. Fraser; The Minority Press, 1933).

no immediately accessible propaganda. Miss Bradbrook, uniting two lines of approach, has found pattern and convention in the poetry itself; and Professor Wilson Knight, by his "mystical" interpretation,[13] again reminds us that Shakespeare was closer to *Everyman* than to *A Doll's House*. I am not attempting anything like a survey of recent criticism. I have said nothing of "verse tests," or of the tendency to split up nearly every play among a number of collaborators and to detect several layers of revision: under the influence of genuinely literary criticism the tide has turned against such misapplication of scientific method. My purpose has been to trace what I consider the most important developments in recent Shakespearean criticism, so as to show how my own work links with that of previous writers. Every approach to Shakespeare has something in it of value, but I am convinced of the fundamental importance of the words themselves— of the poetry—and of the great, though secondary, importance of a knowledge of Elizabethan stage conditions. My own particular approach, considered in these pages, can be undertaken only in the closest association with pure literary criticism and a consideration of Shakespeare's stagecraft.

I have stressed the element of convention in Shakespeare, since it is generally overlooked. But it is necessary also to insist that Shakespeare and his contemporaries worked to no thought-out conventional system; indeed, their conventions are successful just because they are traditional and unconscious. Moreover, being unconscious, they were by no means rigidly adhered to: the Elizabethan playwright varies his position on the scale between conventionalism and naturalism, even in the course of a

[13] See esp. *The Wheel of Fire* (London: Oxford University Press, 1930; reprinted 1937).

single play. This rapidity of adjustment is a principle component in Shakespeare's remarkable subtlety. Lapses into naturalism are especially frequent in Shakespeare: they are probably a major cause of his continuous popularity on the stage, and provide color for a psychological approach which would have failed much more signally with, for example, Chapman or Tourneur. A single flash of natural dialogue, breaking the boundaries of convention, will reveal an intuitive understanding of human nature, unshared by his contemporaries. Othello, filled with the conflicting emotions of love and loathing, visits Desdemona in her chamber, and behaves there as if entering a brothel, calling upon Emilia to perform her "mystery" as doorkeeper. After a tense, but mannered and theatrical, display of passion, he makes an effective exit, still acting his abominable fiction:

> We have done our course; there's money for your pains:
> I pray you, turn the key and keep our counsel.
>
> (IV. ii. 93)

When he has gone out, Emilia addresses her mistress: "How do you, madam? how do you, my good lady?" (IV. ii. 96.) Desdemona's answer is surprising: "'Faith, half asleep" (IV. ii. 97). Within the conventional framework of Elizabethan poetic drama, such a reply is unlikely, and on that account the more arresting. We expect an outburst in keeping with the tone set by Othello, but instead there has been a transition without warning to the plane of naturalism. Tragedy queens seldom complain of fatigue, though there is actually nothing so exhausting as a scene of tense emotion. This sudden revelation of ordinary womanhood in Desdemona engages the audience's sympathy when it is particularly needed, and also points a contrast between her sensible normality and the emotional exaggeration of Othello.

The Elizabethan popular drama made the best of both worlds: its compromise between conventionalism and naturalism is effective because completely unself-conscious. When Shakespeare writes of his art, he is either severely practical as in Hamlet's advice to the players, or he speculates upon the nature of poetry, which

> . . . gives to airy nothing
> A local habitation and a name.
> (*A Midsummer Night's Dream*, V. i. 16)

We never hear from him of the rules of dramatic composition. There is neither the classical pride in obedience, nor the romantic impatience of restraint. There is, indeed, only the most oblique recognition that such matters are under contemporary discussion: *The Tempest* seems to glance aside somewhat whimsically at the neo-Aristotelians. Controversy in dramatic criticism was remarkably one-sided in Elizabethan times, and it came from the side which, on the whole, did not produce memorable plays. Gentlemen amateurs of the Inns of Court, for example, had time to interest themselves in Continental Renaissance criticism and in the Italian revivals and translations of Seneca and Plautus. *Gorboduc*, the first English tragedy, had resulted from this cultivated preoccupation with the Ancients. It would be absurd to minimize the importance of the Renaissance contribution to Elizabethan drama; it was the grafting of this revived classicism upon the sturdy indigenous stock of miracle plays and interludes which produced the unique dramatic activity of late Elizabethan and Jacobean days. But the Elizabethan drama we still revere and revive remained a popular drama; its writers, willing enough to plunder Renaissance hoards, did not as a rule share the Renaissance attitudes. They certainly felt no obligation to imitate the Ancients, or indeed to do anything but write good plays; and they were too immersed in creation to have time for critical theory. Critical self-consciousness, combined with loyalty to the classics, remained the prerogative of a handful of amateurs, especially those gathered about the Countess of Pembroke and her brother, Sir Philip Sidney, and of a relatively small group of professionals who looked to them for patronage. Ben Jonson was the only great figure to combine a measure of practical success with this concern for classical purity; and even Jonson, though his critical theory permitted him success in the field of intellectual comedy, failed in the attempt to write "classical" tragedies which would compete with those of the popular theater. *Gorboduc,* however historically important, has little intrinsic worth; and from *Gorboduc* to *Sejanus,* and on again to the *Catos* and *Irenes* of the eighteenth century, we have a sequence of tragedies, all classically correct and all intolerably dull—a melancholy tale of artistic, and usually of practical, failure. The popular drama had absorbed everything classical that it could translate into terms of the popular tradition, and had ignored the rest. The purists, on the other hand, persisted in their attempt to substitute by violence an alien mode for the unconsciously matured tradition of the popular theater; but their fervor for a more than Aristotelian strictness never ousted the popular tradition as it did in France. Nevertheless, we may say that in Elizabethan times there were two "schools" of drama: the popular school, who had little conscious devotion to a common cause, and made no attempt at dramatic criticism; and the neoclassical school, who, if negligible in the theater, were sufficiently energetic in propaganda for the "rules."

At this stage the popular school was guilty of lapses into naturalism, which the deliberate consistency of the neoclassicals would never allow. And yet it was the neo-classical school which, principally because of its critical self-consciousness, gradually evolved into naturalism of the Ibsen-Pinero type. Neoclassical criticism insisted on its overstrict interpretation of Aristotle, especially in the famous matter of the "unities," but from the beginning its mode of arguing points forward to the naturalistic position. Sidney's famous *Apology for Poetry*, though not printed until after 1595, was "certainly written before 1583,"[14] and so was in the field well before the great efflorescence of popular drama, which it condemns in advance. Sidney's first mention of the theater is reassuring, when he asks rhetorically: "What child is there that, coming to a play, and seeing *Thebes* written in great letters upon an old door, doth believe that it is *Thebes?*" There is a valuable admission here that even a child is not "taken in" by the dramatist's efforts at illusion. But when he comes to a more detailed criticism of the contemporary drama, his viewpoint has surprisingly changed; the whole point of his argument is the necessity of the unities to maintain dramatic illusion, the popular conventions governing time and place being too great a strain on the credulity of a cultivated audience. Even *Gorboduc* is deficient, though admittedly written on the classical model:

Our Tragedies and Comedies (not without cause cried out against), observing rules neither of honest civility nor of skilful Poetry, excepting *Gorboduc* (again, I say, of those that I have seen), which notwithstanding, as it is full of stately speeches and well-sounding phrases, climbing to the height of Seneca's style, and as full of notable morality, which it doth most delightfully teach, and so obtain the very end of Poesy, yet in truth it is very

[14] See *Cambridge History of English Literature*, III, 299.

defectious in the circumstances, which grieveth me, because it might not remain as an exact model of all Tragedies. For it is faulty both in place and time, the two necessary companions of all corporal actions. For where the stage should always represent but one place, and the uttermost time presupposed in it should be, both by Aristotle's precept and common reason, but one day, there is both many days, and many places, inartificially imagined. But if it be so in *Gorboduc*, how much more in all the rest, where you shall have Asia of the one side, and Afric of the other, and so many other under-kingdoms, that the player, when he cometh in, must ever begin with telling where he is, or else the tale will not be conceived? Now ye shall have three ladies walk to gather flowers, and then we must believe the stage to be a garden. By and by we hear news of shipwreck in the same place, and then we are to blame if we accept it not for a rock. Upon the back of that comes out a hideous monster, with fire and smoke, and then the miserable beholders are bound to take it for a cave. While in the mean time two armies fly in, represented with four swords and bucklers, and then what hard heart will not receive it for a pitched field? Now, of time they are much more liberal, for ordinary it is that two young princes fall in love. After many traverses, she is got with child, delivered of a fair boy; he is lost, groweth a man, falls in love, and is ready to get another child; and all this in two hours' space: which, how absurd it is in sense, even sense may imagine, and Art hath taught, and all ancient examples justified. . . .

Since this matter of dramatic illusion is fundamental to my thesis, I am quoting at length; it is valuable to have Sidney's criticisms freshly in mind. After explaining the classical method of dramatic construction, he turns to the unity of action:

But beside these gross absurdities, how all their plays be neither right tragedies nor right comedies, mingling kings and clowns, not because the matter so carrieth it, but thrust in clowns by head and shoulders, to play a part in majestical matters. . . .

However arbitrary this may sound, with its assurance regarding "right tragedies" and "right comedies," it is evident that the standard of reference throughout is one of plausibility, or completeness of dramatic illusion. The controversy, virtually begun by Sidney's *Apology*, continued to rage for a couple of centuries—indeed, it is alive today. In the preface to his edition of Shakespeare, Dr. Johnson considered the matter and treated it with characteristic good sense:

The necessity of observing the unities of time and place arises from the supposed necessity of making the drama credible. The criticks hold it impossible, that an action of months and years can be possibly believed to pass in three hours; or that the spectator can suppose himself to sit in the theatre, while ambassadors go and return between distant kings, while armies are levied and towns besieged, while an exile wanders and returns, or till he whom they saw courting his mistress, shall lament the untimely fall of his son. . . .

From the narrow limitation of time necessarily arises the contraction of place. The spectator, who knows that he saw the first act at *Alexandria*, cannot suppose that he sees the next at *Rome*, at a distance to which not the dragons of *Medea* could, in so short a time, have transported him. . . .

Johnson's answer to the critics is beautifully sane:

It is false, that any representation is mistaken for reality; that any dramatick fable in its materiality was ever credible, or, for a single moment, was ever credited. . . .

The truth is, that the spectators are always in their senses, and know, from the first act to the last, that the stage is only a stage, and that the players are only players. They came to hear a certain number of lines recited with just gesture and elegant modulation. The lines relate to some action, and an action must be in some place; but the different actions that complete a story may be in places very remote from each other; and where is the absurdity of allowing that space to represent first *Athens*, and then *Sicily*, which was always known to be neither *Sicily* nor *Athens*, but a modern theatre?

Johnson combats the neoclassical position by denying the completeness of the illusion—as he could very well do in respect of plays written up to that time. Modern naturalism, however, if it has not persuaded the audience entirely to forget the rows of seats in front, the program-sellers, and the orchestra pit, does rely for its effect upon the relatively long periods during which they can be so persuaded. Shakespeare, or any play in the popular tradition, can be enjoyed while it is realized as "only a play," but such consciousness of the play as play would ruin the effect of naturalistic dialogue and production.

The neoclassical aim, then, seems to have been to reduce the strain on the imagination, to render complete the dramatic illusion, and, to this end, to make dramatic representation correspond as closely as possible to reality. Although Sidney and Jonson supported a system of arbitrary conventions more exclusive of naturalism than the unconscious and flexible tradition of popular drama, the true end of this neoclassical striving for completeness of dramatic illusion lies not in Racine, but in Ibsen, in Eugene O'Neill's *Anna Christie*, or, indeed, in the sophisticated naturalism of a modern Broadway "success." Its logical conclusion would be the "slice of life," ultra-photographic representation, from which the creative, ordering mind has been expelled. The neoclassicists were wrong about the need to observe the unities for the sake of plausibility (their mistake arose from an overhasty identification of naturalism with the practice of the Ancients), and the unities are not often observed in the modern naturalistic theater; but the principles which caused the neoclassicists to fight for the unities are the principles of naturalism today. So if neoclassicism failed in its directly Aristotelian phase, it did not die, but suffered a quite consistent transformation into the dramatic naturalism characteristic of the late nineteenth and early twentieth centuries. And the naturalistic position cannot be refuted by a Johnsonian appeal to hard fact; it exists not as the critic's hope, but as a dominant power in the theater. One can only point out its inadequacy as a method of dramatic expression, when compared with the spontaneous complexity of popular drama; and this I hope to do in relation to my main theme.

Meanwhile it is interesting to notice that the process by which neoclassicism passed into dramatic naturalism is only one aspect of a general reorientation of thought and feeling. The Renaissance gave rise to rationalism and to experimental science. By "rationalism" I mean primarily a belief that truth is discoverable only by the conscious processes of the discursive reason, isolated from the mind as a whole. The reason, it was maintained, must be uncolored by emotion and unaided by the imagination; irrational "feelings" and "convictions," "intuition," and the fruits of mere experience must alike be disregarded, whilst divine revelation was more and more suspect. At first rationalism corresponded generally to the critics' assertion of the unities, each maintaining the superiority of conscious thought over unconscious tradition. But the prestige of experimental science was so great in the later seventeenth century that, quite unconsciously, the physical universe as known to science was assumed to possess a degree of certainty superior to the findings of the speculative intellect. Unconscious adjustments of the public mind are frequently ironic: Reason, personified by poetic flattery, was most eulogized in the very period that ruthlessly clipped her wings. The eighteenth century saw the growth of materialism, in which the function of reason became limited to the ordering of physical fact. And later, in the same way, that movement in dramatic criticism, which began with the exaltation of reason, ended in submission to the dictatorship of meaningless physical phenomena. For in the nineteenth century philosophic naturalism reached its consummation in the work of Darwin and the popular writings of Spencer and Huxley; and, corresponding to this, the so-called "realistic" drama of the school of Ibsen usurped the serious theater. Agnosticism could not be propounded, nor *A Doll's House* written, without the aid of reason, but in each instance reason was engaged in a melancholy abrogation of her powers.

This explanation of the growth of naturalism in the theater, associating the process with far-reaching changes in philosophic outlook, may appear to be unnecessarily high-flown. Is it not true that, in point of fact, the Elizabethan drama was conventional because physical conditions—the state of theater-building, scene-painting, and stage machinery—made naturalism impossible; and that, as these physical difficulties were gradually overcome, playwrights availed themselves eagerly of every "technical improvement" in order to represent life more naturalistically upon the stage? This suggestion has an alluring appearance of common sense, but suffers from the same sort of oversimplification which characterizes the Marxian materialist interpretation of history. The brief but eventful history of the motion picture provides no true parallel. The direction of change in the motion picture has certainly been from conventionalism towards naturalism, as technical difficulties have been successively overcome. Jerky action, due to the relatively slow rotation of the camera, was capitalized in the early comedies; and the silent films, as a species of mime, constantly

exaggerated and conventionalized both gesture and movement. "Freak" photography was much exploited at first,
when producers were still very conscious of the film as
"moving pictures"; but now that action can be so faith-
fully reproduced, the tendency is to ignore the means of
production, to forget the "art" of the camera, and to
concentrate upon merely natural effects. With the motion picture, however, except for an occasional enlightened
producer, the aim from the first has been an approximation to naturalism, so far as the actual methods of reproduction are concerned; though, as I shall show later,
the average film is even now highly conventional in
"content." But in the theater, naturalism did not appear as a conscious aim until the nineteenth century, when
it also became the goal of many novelists and painters.
Undoubtedly the physical conditions of Shakespeare's
theater gave rise directly to a number of conventions; but
there were conventions which did not arise immediately
out of these conditions (e. g., the use of verse), and there
were conventions which survived the physical conditions
in which they arose (e. g., soliloquy and aside). Some
conventions, again, are common to all popular literature,
dramatic and other (e. g., the use of clearly recognizable
character-types), and are thus not to be ascribed at all
to physical circumstances. Moreover, increased efficiency
in stage mechanics need not lead to an Ibsen-Pinero type
of stage set: it has equally led to the "flying ballet" of
pantomime, and the revolving stage, which is much employed in conventional productions. There is nothing
against mechanical elaboration in its proper place: the
Masque of Ceres, in *The Tempest*, should be produced
with all the technical skill available; but it is barbarous
to outface the poetry of Shakespeare with a tawdry col-

lection of canvas trees. Had the Elizabethans wanted naturalism, they might have come near it in a number of ways, notably by abandoning verse—and the sort of attitude which allowed lions to roam at large in the Forest of Arden. When we consider the physical conditions of Shakespeare's theater, it is well to remember that, if certain conventions depend upon these conditions, the conditions themselves arose out of an attitude which did not despise conventions. When, as in Chapter II, I refer to physical conditions as mediating certain attitudes to dramatic illusion, it must be understood that I do not suggest either historical or logical priority for the conditions; we are back, in fact, with the old problem of the hen and the egg. It is significant that in Italy, where the influence of neoclassicism was strongest, stage sets were constructed in perspective, while the "circus" type of production was still normal in England. It is, of course, possible that, so far as they thought about it all, the Elizabethans did aim consciously at what they conceived to be dramatic naturalism; but, if so, their conception of naturalism must have differed so widely from our own, as still to demand the explanation I have already given in terms of a changing "climate of thought."

Despite a revival of symbolism and recent middle-brow flirtations with the "morality," naturalism still dominates the "serious" theater. The popular theater, however, has never abandoned the popular tradition; music hall, pantomime, revue, and musical comedy, together with the average purely commercial Hollywood film, require of an audience the same basic attitudes to dramatic illusion as a medieval "miracle" or a play of Shakespeare. This is not a veiled appeal for commercial entertainment: I do not suggest that *Rose Marie,* or its most recent equivalent, is as good as *As You Like It* and better than *A Doll's House*. I am not concerned with relative value at all—though if I were, I might hint at the superiority of the unsophisticated "gangster" or "Western" film to the theater of Mr. Priestley and Miss Sayers. Modern popular entertainment, however, differs from the Elizabethan in being more calculatedly commercialized; it is also depraved in values, superficial in ideas, false in sentiment, and insensitive to the quality of words. This is due in particular to the neoclassical—later naturalistic—influence in criticism and the theater, which gradually lured the best minds away from the popular tradition. In general it is a part of the cultural decline consequent upon the triumph of Renaissance attitudes. What is even more serious, materialism, middle-brow psychological drama, the craze for scene painting, and the motion picture's habitual use of natural settings, have all tended to undermine the creative naïveté of the popular audience. Men are, however, more readily corrupted in their desires than altered in their modes of apprehension; and the essential psychology of the popular audience seems perennially the same, except that the capacity to cope with verbal subtlety has largely disappeared under the welter of modern appeals to eye and ear.

What, then, is the essence of this popular dramatic tradition—of the perennial psychology of the popular audience? Miss Bradbrook has a hint of it:

The Elizabethans liked the villain-hero, the ambiguous character who excited paradoxical feelings, and with whom a limited identification was possible. Hence the absurdity of approaching Vindice as a "fallen angel," or a "blasted splendour"; a Miltonic Satan to whom a single mixed response is given. His two sides must be seen separately, as Marston's Antonio saw Julio's two natures, and loved him while he carved him up, or as Othello kissed Desdemona ere he killed her:

> ". . . O thou weed
> That art so lovely fair, and smell'st so sweet."

The two views are held simultaneously and yet quite separately in his mind with a terrifying clearness, and yet they are irreconcilable. It is this which makes their peculiar intensity; it deepens them both, like the juxtaposition of complementary colours. Hamlet has a rather similar feeling about his mother:

> ". . . Sense sure you have,
> Else could you not have motion."
>
> (III. iv. 71)

Dissociation is at its simplest and strongest in Spenser: the Bower of Bliss is described and demolished with equal gusto; the gusto, in fact, largely depends on this reconciliation of opposites.[15]

I cannot agree with Miss Bradbrook's individual judgments. Spenser would have been a greater poet had he reconciled the "æsthetic" values of the Bower of Bliss with its allegorical significance; as it is, unconscious and conscious attitudes pull him different ways. Further, I cannot rest content with an interpretation of character which makes no attempt to unify apparently irreconcilable characteristics. Miss Bradbrook seems to be following Professor Stoll into a complete denial of the relevance of psychology to characterization in drama and fiction. I shall take up this whole matter in due course.[16] Meanwhile, though I doubt its existence in the connections named by Miss Bradbrook, she has at least adumbrated a capacity of the Elizabethan audience, which I regard as fundamentally important: the ability to keep simultaneously in mind two opposite aspects of a situation. The pleasure apparently aroused in the Elizabethan theater

[15] *Elizabethan Stage Conditions*, p. 93.
[16] See Chapter IV, esp. for Stoll, pp. 91-92.

by a concurrence of seeming incompatibles is obviously related to the vogue of "conceited" writing, especially as practiced by the so-called "metaphysical" poets; it is worth remembering that the important works of Shakespeare were contemporary with the secular poetry of John Donne. The conscious delight in paradox evinced by the Elizabethans and Jacobeans is a conscious assertion of the Christian tradition, assailed by new Renaissance attitudes.   Later, with the triumph of neoclassicism, metaphor and conceit were simplified to the deliberate parallelism of simile, whilst naturalism crystallizes expression on the level of events—the "reporting" level, which makes its first unmistakable appearance in the novels of Defoe.   Christianity, however, is founded upon the tension of opposites: God and man, nature and supernature; its doctrines define an union without confusion, between the spiritual and material.   Indeed, any profound reading of experience calls naturally for paradoxical statement.   The Elizabethan audience was perhaps especially receptive to this quality of experience, since it was consciously stressed in those times; but the basic psychological tensions I am to consider are largely unconscious and common to the popular theater in every age.   This partly reflects the Christian origin of postclassical drama, but even more, I think, reveals a tension fundamental to the nature of experience itself.

Instances of this trait, less equivocal than Miss Bradbrook's, may be discovered even in the field of character representation.   Characters, without being themselves made up of incompatible qualities, may evoke distinct and separate responses from the audience.   Thus Falstaff is (a) amusing, and (b) morally reprehensible; an Elizabethan audience would applaud his wit, but approve his final dismissal.   Victorian critics, however, displayed bitter resentment, not only against Henry, but against Shakespeare himself, for refusing to sentimentalize. Where the Victorian critic laughs, he must love; but a popular audience is never under this necessity. In the miracle plays, humor was mainly provided by Herod and the fiends, characters held in abhorrence; similarly the Vice of the moralities was forerunner of the Shakespearean clown (does this account for a certain malignity in Feste?); and the pantomime audience today still laughs at the discomfiture of a comic devil. Not only character, but every aspect of the Elizabethan drama, is shot through with this quality of dual awareness. The mixture of conventionalism and naturalism demands a dual mode of attention. Awareness of the play as play implies the dual awareness of play world and real world: upon this depends the piquancy of a play-within-the-play, or of the situation in which a boy plays the part of a girl playing the part of a boy (Julia, Jessica, Rosalind, Viola, Imogen, Perdita). And the Elizabethan apparently enjoyed a song, when it broke the continuity of the play, perhaps criticizing the performer's voice ("A mellifluous voice" (*Twelfth Night*, II. iii. 54)) before taking up the play again where he dropped it for the counterattraction of music.

The modern moviegoer has a similar adaptability. It is not unusual for characters in an apparently "straight" film to break into song, although the circumstances, considered naturalistically, would practically forbid such behavior. A pair of lovers steal away from the company, discover a convenient garden-seat, and, after some preliminary conversation, break into a love-duet, to the accompaniment of an unseen orchestra. Even those little conversant with the etiquette of high society must be aware that this is an unusual method of proposing marriage. As the film setting is naturalistic, the strain upon credulity is correspondingly great, but I have noticed few traces of my own uneasiness in other members of the audience. It is not stupidity, but absence of technical sophistication, which can so rapidly accept a situation as conventional. In this instance, story is accepted as story, and song as song, simultaneously yet without confusion; and none of the awkward questions are asked which would result from a monistic attitude to dramatic illusion. The co-presence of song and story is the commonest example of an audience's ability to sustain two aspects of a situation at once: in opera, it is called for continuously, and Shakespeare's comedies are nearer in this respect to modern musical comedy than to the plays, say, of Galsworthy or Barrie. In the average Hollywood film, conventionalism and naturalism are deeply interwoven. Setting and presentation are usually naturalistic, but characters conform to well-known types, stories follow a recognized pattern, and startlingly unrealistic incidents may be introduced; indeed, criticism is usually leveled at "slapstick" in serious films, much as neoclassical criticism objects to the mixture of comedy and tragedy in Shakespeare. Even in the motion picture there are quite complicated instances of an audience's ability to attend simultaneously to various aspects of a situation. In one of Mr. Harold Lloyd's comedies, a number of years ago, the comedian performed a series of hair-raising evolutions on the front and very near the top of a formidable skyscraper. The audience must have had several concurrent reactions: (a) they would admire the performance of a brilliant "equilibrist"; (b) they would be amused at his (recognizedly feigned) clumsiness; and (c) they would be concerned for the hero's safety, in sympathy with the heroine watching anxiously from below. The same incident demands attention from three different points of view simultaneously: as equilibristic performance, as farce, and as romance. And the audience responds in this complex way without conscious effort. This is the core of my present thesis: that a popular audience, uncontaminated by abstract and tendentious dramatic theory, will attend to several diverse aspects of a situation, simultaneously yet without confusion.

That the playwright should avail himself of this fact is a prerequisite of all dramatic subtlety. Conditions in the Elizabethan theater were ideal. Shakespeare's Globe was a truly national theater, with the cultural stratification one of degree only—not of kind, as it is today; and the playwright, who was presumably producer also, and frequently an actor in the company, would find himself in an intimate relationship with an unified and habitual audience. Such an atmosphere would favor spontaneous development. Conventions would exist, not as a conscious systematization of the playwright, but as an unconscious and organic outgrowth of playhouse psychology; a body of traditional assumptions held in common by playwright and audience. Mr. T. S. Eliot disapproves of the Elizabethan tendency to fluctuate between conventionalism and naturalism,[17] but this very tendency reveals the plasticity of unself-conscious art. It is the countertendency, first observable in Sidney's still curiously respected essay, which has proved disastrous. The imposition of rigid external rules, with an intention of eliminating the improbable, simplified the process of attention to one level throughout a play: farce no longer mingled with tragedy in the neoclassical theater, while the introduction of popular songs, or a wrestling match (as in *As You Like It*),

---

[17] See *Selected Essays:* "The art of the Elizabethans is an impure art" (p. 114).
"What is fundamentally objectionable is that in the Elizabethan drama there has been no firm principle of what is to be postulated as a convention and what is not" (p. 115).

would have outraged the new proprieties. Neoclassicism having declined into naturalism, the proper term of its process of simplification, it is to the despised popular theater that we must look for a revival of the drama, since only there do the rudiments survive of an appropriate psychological situation. Isolated writers and the artificial efforts of repertory can achieve little, for a flourishing drama is the epiphenomenon of a flourishing and organic national culture. There is one recent play which may be a "sport" (as biologists say) or perhaps the forerunner of revival. *Murder in the Cathedral*, with its complex demands upon the audience, is the nearest modern approach to serious art in the popular tradition. Mr. Eliot has significantly written in praise of the old music hall, and in this play he exploits music-hall devices in the service of the highest dramatic aims. If this be inconsistent with his judgment upon the Elizabethans, it is a blessed inconsistency.

To sum up, I believe I am justified in asserting that there *is* a popular dramatic tradition, and that its dominant characteristic is the audience's ability to respond spontaneously and unconsciously on more than one plane of attention at the same time. I shall call this the principle of multiconsciousness. Already, with the aid of some recent critics, we have discovered traces of the operation of this principle in the plays of Shakespeare, and we have found the same principle to hold of the popular theater and motion picture of today. In my remaining chapters I propose to consider some of the problems of Shakespearean criticism in the light of the principle of multiconsciousness, making use from time to time of parallels from the modern theater and motion picture, whenever they seem helpful. The reactions of an Elizabethan audience have always been a matter of speculation, but if the

Elizabethan and the modern popular audiences have the principle of multiconsciousness in common, argument from present to past should be rather more than analogical. The process is, I think, more justifiable and less hazardous than the anthropologist's habit of arguing from the decadent savage of today to the state of primitive man. Our modern audience has little susceptibility to words, and is less inclined than the Elizabethans to seek out symbolic or allegorical significances; while the whole influence of an immorally mechanized civilization tends to the decay of constructive imagination. Yet the popular tradition has survived, and the parallel between modern and Elizabethan popular drama is in some respects sufficiently close to warrant our attention.

CHAPTER II

PLANES OF REALITY*

THERE is no need to summarize what is known of the
structure and physical conditions of the Elizabethan theater, since this has been well done by a number of writers.
It is necessary, however, to stress certain relevant factors.[1]
As galleries ran all round the theater, even above the
back of the stage, the actors could be seen from every
direction, as in a circus. Below them, in the roofless yard,
groundlings crowded close on three sides of the projecting
"apron"; whilst even more embarrassing was the prox-
imity of those young men of fashion who, hiring stools
upon the stage itself, displayed their own rich costume in
competition with the company's wardrobe. Even with the
abundance of make-up, scenery, and properties in use today, it would have been impossible for actors so closely
beset with audience, to create and sustain an illusion of
actual life, especially as they performed in broad daylight.
In Shakespeare's time painted scenery was, in fact, used
hardly at all; and since the "act drop" was still unknown,
stools, benches, and other properties must have been
carried on and off in full sight of the audience; beds, we
know, were directed to be "thrust out" on to the stage,
complete with occupant. A small set might be prepared
on the "inner stage" behind a drawn curtain; but this was
possible only for scenes of small dimension, such as the

---

* I have taken this term, and with it a valuable suggestion, from
Shakespeare's Last Plays, by E. M. W. Tillyard (London: Chatto &
Windus, 1938).

[1] My facts are taken from E. K. Chambers, *The Elizabethan Stage*
(4 vols., Oxford: Clarendon Press, 1923), from *Shakespeare and the
Theatre*, and from the works of Miss Bradbrook already named.

Capulets' tomb, or Belarius' cave in *Cymbeline*. In these circumstances, much of the "business" was necessarily conventional: a siege was represented by an attack upon the "tiring house," with scaling ladders erected against the gallery above. There was some crude realism, and a scene of violent death might be rendered more convincing by pricking a bladder of vinegar (presumably beneath the victim's shirt), as is directed in the pre-Shakespearean *Cambises;* Shakespeare himself seems to have discarded such obvious methods after his early experimental plays. The sort of realism represented by a fully furnished drawing-room set in Ibsen or Pinero was, of course, unattainable and seems hardly to have been desired. The Elizabethans relied on their poetry for much that is nowadays left to the producer. Though more subtly efficient than our modern stage mechanism in securing the appropriate responses, the use of verse in itself marks a further remove from naturalism. Verse goes with conventionalism, whilst naturalism logically implies a colloquial prose. This accounts for the inappropriateness of Victorian productions of Shakespeare, where naturalistic settings conflicted with the subtler atmospheric suggestions of the verse.

The inability of the Elizabethan theater to produce an illusion of actuality was wholly to the good, as modern experimental theaters have shown. At a standard presentation of Ibsen, the audience remain passively receptive, whilst in another, two-dimensional world, beyond the orchestra pit, within a picture frame, and behind footlights, the actors create a vivid illusion of actual life. In the Elizabethan or the modern experimental theater, there is no illusion of actual life; but the audience are vividly aware of acting in progress and the communication, through their co-operative goodwill, of a work of dramatic art.   If the one type of production is more realistic, the other is essentially more real.

Shakespeare, despite an occasional grumble at the inadequacy of his "wooden O" (*Henry V*, Prologue, l. 13) wisely accepted the situation as it was, and turned it to good.   Perhaps he would have welcomed the resources at Ibsen's command, but fortunately he was safe from temptation.   I do not suggest that he had any conscious insight into the advantages of his own position; indeed, its strength lay partly in the unconscious acceptance, by both playwright and audience, of conditions as they found them.   But Shakespeare did not merely acquiesce in those limitations which the physical conditions of his theater placed upon dramatic illusion; he actually exploited them, so that conventions in production are integrally related to conventions in the treatment of history, in the presentation of character, and in the verse.   Moreover, he even draws attention to the play as play, overtly, in the dialogue itself, emphasizing verbally what the manner of production already implied: the co-existence of play world and real world in the minds of his audience.   Perhaps when characters within a play referred to plays and players or noted that "All the world's a stage" (*As You Like It*, II. vii. 139), a certain piquancy in the situation may have been all that forced itself into conscious attention.   Since they had never experienced naturalistic drama, the Elizabethans would not appreciate, as we do today, the nature of their own drama in distinction from it; just as it is impossible to appreciate a state of physical well-being until suffering has supplied us with a standard of comparison.   But this double consciousness of play world and real world has the solid advantage of "distancing" a play, so that the words and deeds of which it consists may be critically weighed in the course of its performance. An Ibsen drama, attended to passively, is discussed afterwards in abstract terms; but in a Shakespearean play, criticism is an integral part of apprehension, and apprehension thereby becomes an activity of the whole mind. This is, of course, due mainly to the fact that the verse must be understood for a proper appreciation of the action; but the detachment necessary for attention to the verse is gained by insisting on the essential artificiality of the play world, and thus holding play world and real world before the mind simultaneously yet without confusion. Such an attitude has the advantage of accepting and exploiting the situation as it really is, whereas naturalism must engage in a constant effort to delude the audience into taking for actuality what they are bound to know, in their moments of critical alertness, to be only a stage performance. To gain a hearing, naturalism destroys the critical awareness necessary for appreciation; it is hardly surprising that a method thus divided against itself has produced little of permanent value.

When Malvolio appears before Olivia's household, cross-gartered and in "the trick of singularity" *(Twelfth Night*, II. v. 164*)*, Signor Fabian has an interesting comment: "If this were played upon a stage now, I could condemn it as an improbable fiction" (III. iv. 140). It is, of course, an improbable fiction, and Shakespeare is employing a common enough literary device to cope with it. There are a great many novelists whose characters exclaim: "Why, it's just like a novel!" This sort of remark carries more than one layer of suggestion. Superficially it makes an improbable situation more plausible. If the characters displayed no consciousness of its improbability, we should be left with a rankling doubt; but since they react as we do to the situation, we are able to accept its improbability and incorporate it into the world of fiction.

At the same time, whatever illusion may have been created has now been broken through: Shakespeare's mention of "playing upon a stage" forcibly reminds his audience of the nature of the spectacle before them.   A naturalistic writer plays with fire when he attempts this sort of thing; but in the Elizabethan theater, with an audience continually aware of the two worlds of fiction and reality side by side, the effect is at the same time to justify an improbable situation and to underline the essential unreality of the play world.   This latter function is much the more important: Shakespeare was not sufficiently concerned for probability and consistency to have inserted Fabian's comment merely for the sake of verisimilitude. It occurs at a significant juncture when the baiting of Malvolio is about to be carried to extremes.   The passage continues:

> *Sir To.:* His very genius hath taken the infection of the device, man.
> *Mar.:* Nay, pursue him now, lest the device take air and taint.
> *Fab.:* Why, we shall make him mad indeed.
> *Mar.:* The house will be the quieter.
> *Sir To.:* Come, we'll have him in a dark room and bound. . . .
> (III. iv. 142)

The Victorians, who sympathized with Malvolio's sufferings to the extent of creating him a tragic hero, and who disdained the Elizabethan crudity which could enjoy Sir Toby's horseplay, failed to perceive that the Elizabethans were not in the habit of mistaking their comedies for real life. Shakespeare erected, through Fabian, a plain enough notice for his audience and for the Victorians too, if they had taken trouble with his text. We are reminded that the play is only a play, just when the reminder is needed to enable us to enjoy the comedy of Malvolio's imprisonment.   The original audience would take such a hint unconsciously, but the Victorians, cut off from the popular tradition, preferred to discover the tragedy which Shakespeare was so careful not to write.

This explanation of Shakespeare's deeper—and surely unconscious—intention may seem far-fetched, and would never have occurred to me had I considered only the passage from *Twelfth Night*. But elsewhere there are similar reminders of the play as play without any ostensible design of rendering plausible an improbable incident. Indeed, in *Love's Labour's Lost*, the immediate intention is diametrically opposite: to excuse a naturalistic departure from the normal theatrical habit of ending a light comedy with wedding bells. *Love's Labour's Lost* is the most artificial of Shakespeare's comedies; the only note of ungarbled seriousness occurs at the end, when Biron is condemned to "jest a twelve-month in an hospital" (V. ii. 881), as a cure for levity and a preliminary to marriage. The unusual task imposed by Rosaline upon her knight breaks incongruously into the abstract gaiety of a simplified play world, bearing a sharp reminder of suffering and sorrow, ingredients of the real world hitherto unheeded through five acts of artificial wit-combat. This bitter reminder of the real world is underlined and at the same time distanced by the ensuing remarks of Biron and the King:

> *Biron:* Our wooing doth not end like an old play;
> Jack hath not Jill: these ladies' courtesy
> Might well have made our sport a comedy.
> *King:* Come, sir, it wants a twelvemonth and a day,
> And then 'twill end.
> *Biron:* That's too long for a play.
>
> (V. ii. 884)

The young Shakespeare, commenting in public on his technique, reinforces the dual consciousness of play world and real world in the minds of his audience. A play so artificial may end quite appropriately with a reference from within to its own true nature. But, coming immediately after the hospital theme, this passage serves a more delicate purpose. With its reminder of reality, as distinguished from the play world, it underlines the reference to human suffering by taking us back to the real world where it is to be encountered. At the same time, by making explicit the nature of the play as play, it preserves a threatened poise: we remember that it is a stage personage only who is to "jest a twelvemonth in an hospital" and that personal sympathy would be misplaced. The intellectual position of the comedy has been strengthened, whilst its "artificiality" has been satisfactorily restored.

In plot and setting, *As You Like It* is every whit as artificial as *Love's Labour's Lost*. There is the same movement of lovers in patterned pairs (with two temporary triangles as an added complication in the later play); and the Masque of Hymen completes a general, if superficial, resemblance to the modern "musical comedy." The dialogue is easy and relatively mature: Rosalind's prose in the Forest of Arden is so natural-seeming that as a character she "comes alive" mainly by this means; but Shakespeare is the more careful to provide a balance of artificiality in his verse and to indicate through his verse technique the varying degrees of actuality to which we are expected to adjust ourselves. This explains the antiphonal echoing of phrases between Orlando and Duke Senior, when the former bursts in upon the exiles with his demand for hospitality:

> *Orl.:* . . . If ever you have look'd on better days,
> If ever been where bells have knoll'd to church,
> If ever sat at any good man's feast,
> If ever from your eyelids wiped a tear
> And know what 'tis to pity and be pitied, ...

Duke S.: True is it that we have seen better days,
 And have with holy bell been knoll'd to church
 And sat at good men's feasts and wiped our eyes
 Of drops that sacred pity hath engender'd: . . . .
        (*As You Like It*, II. vii. 113)

This careful pattern of question and answer distances
and tones down a scene where otherwise emotion might
run too high. The tendency throughout is to pass lightly
over whatever has the potentiality of heightened emotion,
in order, presumably, to keep the intellect unclouded and
to concentrate serious attention upon certain themes: court
versus country, literary pastoral and the clodhopping
rustic, tradition and innovation in rural economy. And
so the love tangle resolves itself at a level of actuality
similar to the average Gilbert and Sullivan opera. The
lovers' repetitive phrases have the effect of "Three little
maids from school":

 Sil.: It is to be all made of sighs and tears;
  And so am I for Phebe.
 Phe.: And I for Ganymede.
 Orl.: And I for Rosalind.
 Ros.: And I for no woman.

        (V. ii. 90)

In the next scene, the lovers pair off appropriately, and
Rosalind is reunited to her father mostly in rhyme and
as an integral part of the Masque of Hymen.

Apart from such obvious instances in which verse
technique is used to distance the dramatic experience, it
would be possible to grade all the verse in an ascending
scale of artificiality, from the broken, vigorous dialogue
of Duke Frederick to the near-burlesque of Silvius and
Phebe. Duke Frederick has the sort of verse which de-
velops in the tragedies:

She is too subtle for thee; and her smoothness,
Her very silence and her patience
Speak to the people, and they pity her.
Thou art a fool: she robs thee of thy name;
And thou wilt show more bright and seem more virtuous
When she is gone. Then open not thy lips:
Firm and irrevocable is my doom
Which I have passed upon her; she is banish'd.

(I. iii. 79)

Contrast:

Sil.: Sweet Phebe, do not scorn me; do not, Phebe;
Say that you love me not, but say not so
In bitterness. The common executioner,
Whose heart the accustom'd sight of death makes hard,
Falls not the axe upon the humbled neck
But first begs pardon: will you sterner be
Than he that dies and lives by bloody drops?

(III. v. 1)

This is rhythmically more regular; the fourth and sixth lines have the pointless inversions of a strained "poetic" style; and the conceit has a certain obvious ingenuity typically Petrarchan. Between the extremes that I have quoted, lies a wide range of delicately perceptible differences in style, all indicating degrees of remoteness from actuality. At this time Shakespeare seems to have been serious in prose—there is more prose than verse in *As You Like It*—and to have used verse mainly to emphasize the conventional. This view of the matter is borne out in a significant remark of Jaques. Orlando enters and addresses Rosalind, who, as Ganymede, has been effectively ridiculing Jaques' melancholy:

Orl.: Good day and happiness, dear Rosalind!
Jaq.: Nay, then, God be wi' you, an you talk in blank verse.

(IV. i. 30)

The incident is, I suppose, explicable in naturalistic terms: Orlando utters an involuntary blank verse line, and the cynical Jaques seizes upon it to make his escape with an implied sneer against the lover. But, in any event, the mention of blank verse by a character draws attention to the play as play, in the same way as the remarks of Fabian and Biron, already discussed. Jaques' Parthian shot goes farther, however, by associating blank verse with the conventions of fashionable wooing, and thus suggesting that the play's artificiality is especially constituted by the verse. We have seen that this is, in fact, true of *As You Like It.*

Deliberate emphasis upon the unreality of the play world is uncommon nowadays. It is still, however, an habitual device of the Marx brothers, those excellent Hollywood comedians, who combine the wildest nonsense with a delicate satirical probing of the defective values in our modern civilization. Their methods are purely conventional, and they require above everything an alert audience, ready to grasp at every word and each significant gesture. It would be fatal for their purpose if the audience were to become emotionally involved in the thin line of romantic story which holds their performance together. In their best film, *Animal Crackers,* which appeared some years ago, there are two direct reminders of the film as film. Groucho forgets the name of the character he represents, and turning to the audience, demands a program: this is complicated by the reference back from film to "legitimate" stage, since programs are not provided in the motion picture theater. At another point in the film he reminds us after a feeble pun, that "You can't expect all the jokes to be good." The effect is the same as in Shakespeare; it reinforces the double consciousness of play world and real world, and

at the same time it distances the play as play and produces intimacy with the audience for the actor as actor
rather than as character.

It has already been observed that the acting of female
parts by boys was further complicated by the frequency
with which the story demanded a male disguise. It is
usually said that the boy would welcome relief for a time
from the embarrassment of his unaccustomed garments
and would probably act the better for being unencum-
bered. Since the investigation of Elizabethan theatrical
conditions opened a new field of conjecture, "practical"
explanations of this kind have been carried to excess. A
boy would soon learn to manage his skirts without thinking of them: girls do, and the talent is unlikely to be
inherited. It is better to seek explanations in the nature
of Shakespeare's sources and in the psychology of an
audience to which the principle of multiconsciousness applies. Probably the situation of "boy playing girl playing boy" pleased in its suggestion of multiple planes of
reality. It would, of course, be a pleasure entirely dependent upon the dual consciousness of play world and
real world. I have seen, at a concert-party performance,
a female impersonator (i. e., a man who habitually plays
women's parts) playing the part of a woman in man's
clothes. A popular audience clearly recognized and enjoyed the unusual situation. Cleopatra's objection to a
Roman triumph:

> . . . I shall see
> Some squeaking Cleopatra boy my greatness
> I' the posture of a whore,
>
> (*Antony and Cleopatra*, V. ii. 219)

effects through dialogue a precisely similar complication
in the planes of reality. Also, as a direct reference to
acting, it performs the same function as the other passages

I have considered, bringing forcibly to mind the duality
of play world and real world. This passage is especially
remarkable, since it occurs in a tragedy and at a moment
of great emotional intensity. Moreover, *Antony and
Cleopatra* comes at the end of the tragic period, when
Shakespeare has learned all there is to learn about his
art. An alert and critically detached audience is implied,
and an attitude to tragedy very different from that to
which we are accustomed.

Children are always fascinated by the notion of infinite regression. I remember a certain biscuit-tin which
always gave me, as a small boy, a distinct sense of the
"numinous." It had on it a picture of a boy holding a
tin just like the real one, and on the tin the boy held
was another picture of a boy holding a tin. The childish
question "And who made God?" betrays a similar interest.
The concern of Shakespeare and the Elizabethans with
"planes of reality" shows not, of course, their childish-
ness, but a healthy preoccupation with the questions men
naturally ask when undeterred by the advances of civilization. The "play-within-the-play," as in *A Midsummer Night's Dream* and *Hamlet,* or the device by which
the main play is presented before a stage audience, as in
The Taming of the Shrew or Kyd's *The Spanish Tragedy,*
further illustrates the same preoccupation. An audience
watches a stage audience watching a play and so becomes
simultaneously aware of three planes of reality. Shakespeare carries the matter farther by his frequent metaphorical use of play and players. To Jaques "All the
world's a stage . . ." (*As You Like It,* II. vii. 139), and
to Macbeth

> Life's but a walking shadow, a poor player
> That struts and frets his hour upon the stage
> And then is heard no more.
>
> (*Macbeth,* V. v. 24)

Contemplation of regression, which produced the parlor games of Viola-Cesario and Hamlet's Mousetrap, has here assumed philosophical significance. The solidity of the first plane of reality, the plane of our terrestrial life, is seen to be illusory. It is significant that in the last fully Shakespearean play the planes of reality appear with most complexity. Prospero says of his Masque of Ceres:

> These our actors,
> As I foretold you, were all spirits and
> Are melted into air, into thin air.
> (*The Tempest*, IV. i. 148)

"On the actual stage," observes Dr. Tillyard, "the masque is executed by players pretending to be spirits, pretending to be real actors, pretending to be supposed goddesses and rustics."[2] And immediately after the revels end, Prospero reminds us that, as his spirit actors have vanished, so

> The cloud-capped towers, the gorgeous palaces,
> The solemn temples, the great globe itself,
> Yea, all which it inherit, shall dissolve
> And, like this insubstantial pageant faded,
> Leave not a rack behind. We are such stuff
> As dreams are made on, and our little life
> Is rounded with a sleep.
> (IV. i. 152)

The world is seen as transient, and therefore insubstantial, whilst a reference to the dream world adds a further complication. It seems as if Shakespeare had deliberately crowded into a few moments of his last play all that can suggest the manifold mystery of experience. Both Jaques and Macbeth employed the play metaphor to express an attitude of cynicism: in Jaques, the cynicism which was a

[2] *Shakespeare's Last Plays*, p. 80.

recognized ingredient of contemporary fashionable melancholy; in Macbeth, the cynicism of a hardened sinner,
who, having rejected the laws of God and man, cut off
from all sympathetic contact with the world outside himself, has become incapable of apprehending meaning in
that world. But Prospero's speech begins:

> You do look, my son, in a moved sort,
> As if you were dismay'd: be cheerful, sir.
>
> (IV. i. 146)

To Prospero, whose "beating mind" (IV. i. 163) achieves
at this moment an insight into reality, the transitoriness
of this world is matter for cheerfulness. We are therefore
justified in pushing the parallel farther, and remembering that, though the actors have faded, as invisible
spirits they still exist; and that from sleep there is
awakening. Sleep, in Shakespeare, is always regarded
as remedial:

> Sleep that knits up the ravell'd sleave of care,
> The death of each day's life, sore labour's bath,
> Balm of hurt minds, great nature's second course,
> Chief nourisher in life's feast. . . .
>
> (*Macbeth,* II. ii. 37)

If, as seems likely, Prospero in his great speech voices
Shakespeare's own conclusions, then this passage, far from
proclaiming the agnosticism of a world-weary artist,
clearly asserts, at the culmination of a lifelong and
unique poetic experience, the existence of an eternal order
behind the relatively trivial and impermanent phenom-
enal world, as the "real" world exists in comparative
stability behind the shadow world of the theater. The
survival of human persons after their sleep of death is
incidentally implied. The final organization of Shakespeare's experience is thus functionally related to the

dual consciousness of play world and real world, characteristic of Elizabethan playhouse psychology. If Shakepeare put the whole of life into his plays, he reciprocally interpreted life in terms of the theater.

AN ADDITIONAL NOTE

I do not know whether the Marx brothers are consciously aware, any more than Shakespeare is likely to have been, that the type of joke discussed on page 37 has an important effect upon the relationship of actors and audience. They have continued to employ it in more recent films with remarkable consistency, and this indicates at least a strong instinctive sense of its usefulness. In *The Marx Brothers Go West* we were told as (I think) the engine driver was being gagged: "This is the best gag in the whole picture," and in *The Big Store,* when the villain is finally unmasked, Groucho exclaims, echoing the average comment from the stalls: "I could have told you in the first reel he was a crook." Other comedians have followed the example of the Marx brothers, and this sort of joke is now frequent. Since it demands an alert response from the audience, this revival of a venerable stage-technique is to be welcomed.

CHAPTER III

ANACHRONISM AND THE TREATMENT OF TIME

ANACHRONISMS have long provided the Shakespearean commentator with a series of easy triumphs. Shakespeare is assumed to have been either ignorant or criminally careless, and the discovery of his lapses has proved an entertaining alternative to genuine criticism. Critics have been perhaps insufficiently awed by the greatness of their subject. With Shakespeare the only safe rule is to try every possible explanation before resorting to an adverse judgment: when he is obviously wrong, it is well to remember that Shakespeare is seldom obvious and to see whether he may not after all be profoundly, if less obviously, right. When Brutus and his fellow conspirators are made to pause and count the clock (*Julius Caesar*, II. i. 192), Shakespeare may or may not have been conscious of historical inaccuracy. There were no striking clocks in Roman times; but the anachronism is justified by its dramatic propriety, and since *Julius Caesar* a striking clock has become indispensable to the conspiratorial night-scene. Even Shakespeare, however, must have been aware that "that rare Italian master, Julio Romano" (*The Winter's Tale*, V. ii. 105), belonged to the Renaissance, not to the ancient world—or, if even that knowledge be denied him, it is hardly likely that, with any desire for historical accuracy, he would have permitted Polixenes, a pre-Christian worshiper of Apollo, to refer to the betrayal of Our Lord by Judas Iscariot (I. ii. 419). We cannot avoid the conclusion that, at any rate sometimes, Shakespeare perpetrated his anachronisms deliberately. Nevertheless, critics have frowned upon them; though they have devoted earnest attention to "contemporary references," apparently without realizing that they are in precisely the same category. Macbeth's porter was familiar with the ways of Jesuit equivocators (II. iii. 9). The passage is frequently noted as "contemporary reference": it is also anachronistic, but no one has seen in it an ignorant antedating of St. Ignatius Loyola. Professor Schücking actually recognizes that many of these anachronisms and contemporary references were quite intentional and characteristic of the popular dramatic tradition; but he seems not to like the tradition, and their significance is lost upon him:

The popular tendency of Shakespeare's art [he says] is above all things evident in the flagrant and intentional anachronisms which he employs to render his art palatable to the public. Such references to the immediate present form part of the stock-in-trade of popular art in all periods of history, in Shakespeare's as well as in our time. . . . This rude interruption of the illusion has no parallel in the serious drama of Ben Jonson and his followers . . . even in this early time such anachronisms must have seemed unbearable to people who were proud of their freshly acquired humanistic learning. . . . It is, indeed, a distinguishing feature of the Renaissance that it brought forth the idea of a correct historical perspective, and one of its chief movements was directed against the simplicity of the Middle Ages, which could see the past only in the light of the present. This was certainly a characteristic of Shakespeare's which the following generation thought itself entitled to treat with derision.[1]

Professor Schücking has done a good work in placing Shakespeare within the popular tradition, but his predilection for naturalism prevents him from stating the position properly and from pursuing its implications.

[1] *Character Problems in Shakespeare's Plays*, pp. 21-22.

Shakespeare, we note, has to "render his art palatable to the public"—a variant upon the usual accusation of "pleasing the groundlings." Yet the average Elizabethan playgoer would seem, both from the plays themselves and from external evidence, to have been in many ways better educated than the average playgoer today;[2] and as to the groundlings, Shakespeare, through Hamlet, told them to their faces what he thought of them: they were "for the most part . . . capable of nothing but inexplicable dumb-shows and noise" (*Hamlet,* III. ii. 12), so that they can hardly have been a major consideration with him. Professor Schücking later speaks of "this rude interruption of the illusion": obviously he thinks of the Elizabethans as attempting, but failing, to secure an illusion of actuality as in the naturalistic theater. From such a viewpoint, deliberate anachronism must imply the abandoning of higher dramatic ends for an immediate crude effect. It is very significant that the same passage goes on to suggest approval of "Ben Jonson and his followers," the neoclassical playwrights, and a preference for the Renaissance attitude to history over the medieval. With preconceptions of this kind, though Professor Schücking can point to the phenomenon of deliberate anachronism and its relation to the popular dramatic tradition, he is incapable of appreciating the true significance of his own discovery.

The Elizabethans were, perhaps, relatively lacking in a sense of history; though the modern mind, warped by popular extensions of the theory of evolution, is not necessarily the best judge of this. There is, I think, less margin of error in assuming the mental processes of all

[2] See L. C. Knights, "Education and the Drama in the Age of Shakespeare," *Criterion,* XI (July, 1932), 599-625; also John Semple Smart, *Shakespeare: Truth and Tradition* (London: Edward Arnold & Co., 1928), chap. vi, pp. 149 f.

civilized human beings to be fundamentally similar, than in the modern popular tendency to confuse the Elizabethan or medieval mind with that of Neanderthal Man. Be this as it may, modern attempts to produce Shakespeare with costume and atmosphere relating to the period of the story, and not to Elizabethan times at all, do less than justice to the subtlety of his dramatic art. Experts have decided[3] that a Globe production of *Macbeth* or of a Roman play would be dressed neither with historical accuracy nor in merely contemporary costume; but that a sort of "fancy dress" would be employed, contemporary in essentials, yet suggestive in detail of the place and period required. We may compare Inigo Jones' costume designs for the court masques or the costumes favored by Renaissance painters of historical subjects. Cleopatra's "Cut my lace, Charmian" (*Antony and Cleopatra*, I. iii. 71) shows that she wore Elizabethan stays, but her costume would have bizarre elements about it, Egyptian enough to a Globe audience, if shocking to the modern Egyptologist. In costume, then, there were contemporary features and historical or pseudo-historical features side by side; and in this respect costume merely symbolizes the Elizabethan play as a whole.

In the popular theater of today, a situation similar to the Elizabethan still survives and ought to shed light upon the psychology of an Elizabethan audience. Musical comedies with period setttings are frequent enough. In the matter of costume they have given way before the general increase of historical information, and the aim is fidelity to history insofar as that is compatible with a maximum of theatrical effectiveness. Anachronisms of the "striking clock" variety are, for the same reason, less

[3] Cf. Harley Granville-Barker, *Prefaces to Shakespeare*, Second Series (London: Sidgwick & Jackson, 1930), pp. 166-167.

frequent and less obvious; but the dialogue still abounds in contemporary reference, especially in the comic roles. In the days when "Yes, We Have No Bananas" was a new and astonishingly popular song, an enterprising amateur comedian utilized it for a "gag" inserted into a performance of *Les Cloches de Corneville.* Local purists who objected on historical grounds had suffered contamination from the naturalistic theater. A popular audience, on the other hand, attends to such a performance on two planes simultaneously: the story is attended to as historical, and the contemporary reference as contemporary. Neither is confused with the other: the popular song is not thought of as being also popular in the eighteenth century, nor is the eighteenth-century character thought of as having a miraculous foreknowledge of twentieth-century jazz music. This variety of dual consciousness is, of course, organically related to, and dependent upon, the dual consciousness of play world and real world. When an illusion of actuality has been created, and the audience inhabits only one world, the play world, contemporary reference is resented as incongruous. But with an audience critically alert to the play as play, not duped into accepting it as if it were real life, the two planes of past history and current affairs can be attended to simultaneously, yet without confusion.

In the Elizabethan theater, apart from the work of the neoclassical group, all historical plays are written in this manner. Here, at least, Shakespeare is bound to have been to some extent aware of what he was doing. He may not have been fully conscious of every anachronism he introduced, but he must have been aware of dealing, in the historical plays, with two ages, his own and some other. The reference to equivocators, for example, cannot have been accidental. In the same way, his audience would be aware of attending to two periods at once. But probably neither Shakespeare nor his audience would be self-consciously aware of this dual awareness, as being only one method of dealing with historical material. Simplification to the single historical level, far from being natural, results entirely from the preconceptions of neoclassical and naturalistic criticism.

The modern procedure in writing historical plays for the "serious" theater weights the playwright with intolerable chains. Not only must he secure the greatest accuracy in matters of fact, but he must endeavor to be faithful to period in portraying the minds of his characters: he must not allow them to think in terms of a later period, or even to use metaphor derived from a mode of life which would actually be unknown to them.[4] This means that a writer of historical plays must shut out from his mind a good seventy-five per cent of his experience—the most detailed and original part of it, which he has gained in commerce with contemporary life. His writing becomes bookish and thin, and he tends to affect a style of imitation antiquity. His play, when produced, probably achieves the illusion of actuality for something abstract and remote, which has only the most general connection with contemporary life. Shakespeare, on the other hand, is able to use all the richness of his contemporary experience in writing of the past. For it is not only in "anachronisms" and occasional references that contemporary life enters into an Elizabethan historical play; in the style there is no attempt at all to preserve historical perspective, and the imagery, often clearly contemporary and "out of period," assures continuity of sharp contrast between the historical material and the

---

[4] Shaw is an exception here, but there is nothing naturalistic in his theater.

contemporary experience with which it is brought into active relationship.   The co-presence of such contrasting elements renders doubly impossible any mere illusion of actuality; once again, the audience must necessarily remain critically alert, whilst at the same time the historical element distances and objectifies what is contemporary, and the contemporary element gives current significance to an historical situation. The equivocators, for example, had conspired to kill the king, as Macbeth was doing; and Macbeth's own regicide involved him in a life of equivocation.   The whole atmosphere of treason and distrust which informs *Macbeth* found a parallel in the England of the Gunpowder Plot, so that a passing reference serves to define an attitude both to the Macbeth regime and to contemporary affairs. The limitations of Professor Schücking are well illustrated by his comment on the Porter incident: "One might as well to-day interrupt the performance by reading the latest edition of the evening papers to the audience."[5]

It is clear, from the chronicle plays and from every other play where such subjects are touched on, that Shakespeare had a philosophy of history. His reverence for the anointed king and consequent horror at usurpation, his regard for order and distrust of the common people as a factor in politics, have been discussed by generations of critics. His treatment of the house of Lancaster consistently reveals the divine punishment of an usurping line, a punishment necessarily shared by the country at large, since king and country are organically one:

> The blood of English shall manure the ground,
> And future ages groan for this foul act,
>
> (*Richard II*, IV. i. 137)

[5] *Op. cit.*, p. 24.

the Bishop of Carlisle prophesies, in *Richard II*; and before Agincourt, Henry V remembers his father's crime:

> Not to-day, O Lord,
> O, not to-day, think not upon the fault
> My father made in compassing the crown!
> *(Henry V*, IV. i. 309)

It is not merely that Shakespeare takes his plots from history; he is concerned to interpret history, though in terms of the political philosophy of his own day. His political beliefs are the common beliefs of Tudor England: on the stage they had been expressed long before in *Gorboduc,* which asserts the necessity of a strong hereditary monarchy to preserve order and due subordination in the state and covertly urges upon the Queen that it is her duty to delay no longer in establishing the succession. There is direct evidence that the young Shakespeare studied his *Gorboduc,* and particularly the long final speech whose pedagogical monotony must have irritated Her Majesty no less than its presumptuous advice. A woeful picture is presented of the desolation of "Brittaine realme" when "left an open pray"[6] through the failure of the royal line. Amongst a great many other calamities, we hear that

> With fire and sworde thy natiue folke shall perishe;
> One kinsman shall bereaue an-others life;
> The father shall vnwitting slay the sonne;
> The sonne shall slay the sire, and know it not.
> *(V. ii. 211)*

---

[6] *Gorboduc,* V. ii. 191, in *Chief Pre-Shakespearean Dramas,* ed. J. Q. Adams (London: George G. Harrap & Co., n. d.), p. 533.

The list concludes with a comment: "These be the fruites your ciuil warres will bring" (V. ii. 233). When Shakespeare, at the beginning of his career, wrote of the Wars of the Roses, he remembered his *Gorboduc* and introduced into a battle scene in *King Henry VI, Part III* (*III Henry VI*, II. v) two characters described in stage directions as "*a* Son *that has killed his father*" and "*a* Father *that has killed his son.*"   The deed has been done unwittingly in each instance, directly recalling the "prophetic" speech in *Gorboduc*.   Shakespeare, then, in the orthodox line of Tudor political philosophy, brings history into active relationship with contemporary life; he does not immerse himself in the past, but contemplates the past in the light of his own times.   This is the attitude which Professor Schücking deprecated as "medieval." But Tudor England remained medieval in the deeper strata of its culture; the Renaissance fired a general enthusiasm, but its new attitudes did not at first strike deep.   The question of the succession and the possibility of civil war and usurpation exercised the politically minded in Elizabethan England.   In his chronicle plays Shakespeare treats these very themes, not only in the Lancastrian sequence, but in *King John;* and the same concern is echoed here and there in the later plays, especially in *Troilus and Cressida, Macbeth,* and *The Tempest,* as political philosophy gradually takes its place in a symbolic interpretation of the univerce.

With his views of kingship and the political order, it is natural that Shakespeare should have treated history as centering in the king and the great nobles. It is also dramatically convenient to personalize history in this way.   In the chronicle plays, events and philosophical speculation upon them are more important than questions of character.   The great personages are presented in bare outline: they are hypostatizations of political standpoints, with little human detail. Even so, there is usually an attempt to give them the characteristics ascribed to them by history and tradition. A popular audience dislikes the reversal of traditional judgments: *Troilus and Cressida* casts doubt upon chivalric values, but even here Shakespeare preserves the Trojans' moral superiority, which medieval romance had always asserted, following the Roman bias. However inaccurate by modern standards, Shakespeare's history is faithful to the broad facts as they were understood in Elizabethan times: he may compress and alter for his immediate dramatic ends, but he does not deliberately distort what he believes to be the truth. In addition, however, the chronicle plays also contain important elements drawn directly from contemporary life. This does not imply a sporadically frivolous disregard of historical consistency, but is the technical fulfilment of a philosophy of history which always regards the past in the light of current affairs. The Bastard in *King John* is presented with some care, yet he is wholly a figure of the Renaissance. In his "Commodity" speech we have the cynicism which Elizabethan playwrights understood to be the teaching of Machiavelli:

> And why rail I on this Commodity?
> But for because he hath not woo'd me yet:
> Not that I have the power to clutch my hand,
> When his fair angels would salute my palm;
> But for my hand, as unattempted yet,
> Like a poor beggar, raileth on the rich.
> Well, whiles I am a beggar, I will rail
> And say there is no sin but to be rich;
> And being rich, my virtue then shall be
> To say there is no vice but beggary.
> Since kings break faith upon commodity,
> Gain, be my lord, for I will worship thee.
>
> (*King John*, II. i. 587)

The earlier "Brother, adieu" speech, after his knighthood has been conferred, reveals him as a typical "new man," a social climber, grasping at wealth and position:

> Well, now can I make any Joan a lady.
> "Good den, Sir Richard!"—"God-a-mercy, fellow!"—
> And if his name be George, I'll call him Peter;
> For new-made honour doth forget men's names;
> 'Tis too respective and too sociable
> For your conversion. Now your traveller,
> He and his toothpick at my worship's mess,
> And when my knightly stomach is sufficed,
> Why then I suck my teeth and catechize
> My picked man of countries: "My dear sir,"
> Thus, leaning on mine elbow, I begin,
> "I shall beseech you"—that is question now;
> And then comes answer like an Absey book:
> "O sir," says answer, "at your best command;
> At your employment; at your service, sir:"
> "No sir," says question, "I, sweet sir, at yours:"
> And so, ere answer knows what question would,
> Saving in dialogue of compliment,
> And talking of the Alps and Apennines,
> The Pyrenean and the River Po,
> It draws towards supper in conclusion so.
> But this is worshipful society
> And fits the mounting spirit like myself. . . .
>   (I. i. 184)

Elizabethan society was plagued with *nouveaux riches,* who bought up the estates of impoverished gentry and played the coxcomb at aldermen's feasts or hung tentatively upon the fringes of the court. It was fashionable for such an individual to travel Europe; and satire upon the returned traveler is common in Elizabethan literature: later Rosalind twits Jaques with having "sold his own land to see other men's" (*As You Like It,* IV. i. 22).

The Bastard is hardly a character; he shifts his function from scene to scene and can even become the mouthpiece of English patriotic defiance. But as bastard, he is a fitting companion for the usurper, John; and as a contemporary figure, the *parvenu* tainted with Machiavellian notions, he links the disorder of an usurper's reign to the subtler social *malaise* of Elizabethan times, which proceeded from the uncontrolled growth of commercial enterprise and the dissemination of a secular and individualistic philosophy. In this way, "anachronism" becomes fruitful in implied judgments upon both past and present.

It is in the two parts of *King Henry IV* that past and present are most obviously brought together. On the one hand we have high politics, more or less correct historically, and on the other, the Falstaff material, drawn entirely from the "low life" of contemporary London and the middling life of the shires. In the dialogue of Falstaff and his companions, references to the theater are especially prominent. Falstaff himself begins his burlesqued King Henry "in King Cambyses' vein" (*I Henry IV*, II. iv. 425), and then modulates into a characteristically Lylyan prose; while Pistol's dialogue is built up throughout of misquotation from contemporary drama of every quality. All this exactly parellels the reference to "Yes, We Have No Bananas," intruded into a performance of *Les Cloches de Corneville*. Falstaff, again, has the taste of a wealthy Elizabethan merchant: "Glasses, glasses, is the only drinking: and for thy walls, a pretty slight drollery, or the story of the Prodigal, or the German hunting in water-work, is worth a thousand of these bed-hangings and these fly-bitten tapestries" (*II Henry IV*, II. i. 155).

More important, his recruiting methods were only too frequent under Queen Elizabeth: "Shadow will serve for summer; prick him, for we have a number of shadows to fill up the muster-book" (III. ii. 144). Falstaff, that is, had more names on his roll than men in his service and appropriated the pay of these "shadows" to himself. This setting back of contemporary abuses into history serves to distance and objectify them. It is the same principle which inspired Swift to diminish and increase the human stature in order to reveal human failings the more clearly. We are ready enough to condemn the actions of beings sufficiently remote; but scarcely has judgment been passed, when we realize that the same deeds are normally condoned among ourselves and that our judgment is, in effect, self-accusation. Falstaff's callousness towards his enlisted rabble stands out from its framework of history: "Tut, tut; good enough to toss; food for powder, food for powder; they'll fill a pit as well as better: tush, man, mortal men, mortal men" (*I Henry IV*, IV. ii. 71). The blurred outlines of a contemporary abuse have been sharpened by transferring it from a familiar to an unfamiliar setting. Conversely, there might seem to be little of interest to an Elizabethan audience in the confused series of rebellions against King Henry IV; but presented with a background of vividly contemporary life, they gain in reality and significance. Falstaff, a "modern" man enough, is drawn into the wars, and his views of military honor effectively counter the literary-romantic notions put into the mouth of Hotspur. Hotspur would "pluck bright honour from the pale-faced moon" (I. iii. 202). Although in the last century considered poetical, the line is meaningless rant—and Shakespeare does not write meaningless rant without intending to. We must take its sound and fury as an evaluation of the romantic glory associated with war. Hotspur is seldom taken seriously, certainly not by Prince Hal, whom we must clearly accept as hero:

I am not yet of Percy's mind, the Hotspur of the north; he that kills me some six or seven dozen of Scots at a breakfast, washes his hands, and says to his wife "Fie upon this quiet life! I want work." "O my sweet Harry," says she, "How many hast thou killed to-day?" "Give my roan horse a drench," says he; and answers "Some fourteen," an hour after; "a trifle, a trifle."

(II. iv. 114)

The "strong, silent man" was not *persona grata* with Shakespeare and the Elizabethans. Falstaff on the battlefield provides the best antidote to Hotspur's enthusiasm:

Can honour set to a leg? no: or an arm? no: or take away the grief of a wound? no. Honour hath no skill in surgery, then? no. What is honour? a word. What is in that word honour? what is that honour? air. . . .

(V. i. 133)

It is *flatus vocis*, as the extreme nominalists would have said. This, of course, is as one-sided a view as that of Hotspur: but it indicates the reactions of a "modern" un-heroic individual, drawn into the alien environment of civil war. Through Falstaff, who all along had been strictly a contemporary figure, the audience, instead of regarding Hotspur's heroics in remote complacency, were forced to realize the civil war situation as a present pos-sibility and to consider the very different code which in such circumstances they themselves might be tempted to apply. The present is thus distanced and appraised, and the past made uncomfortably alive by this duality of time which characterizes the Shakespearean treatment of history.

In his tragic period, Shakespeare used the same method for subtler purposes. I have already mentioned the "equivocator" passage in *Macbeth*; but apart from the Porter speech and "prophetic" acclamation of the Stuarts, contemporary reference and anachronism are here limited to the imagery ("As cannons overcharged with double cracks" (*Macbeth*, I. ii. 37)), and to the broad theme of individual ambition *versus* traditional religious sanctions, which reflects the Elizabethan struggle between medieval and Renaissance attitudes. Complex consciousness within the story itself relates mainly to the natural and supernatural orders and to the double status of the latter as (a) objective and (b) symbolical of subjective states. Thus the "air-drawn dagger" is probably a vision sent by fiends—in Elizabethan times this was a common and traditional explanation of such phenomena[7] —and a dramatic symbol, perhaps also a projection, of Macbeth's own consciousness. This ambiguity of subjective and objective further reflects the sinner's uncertain grasp of objective reality, which results from setting up the private universe of his own supposed good, in opposition to the real universe as divinely ordered.

King Lear, however, is the tragedy which makes most use of the contrast between historical period and contemporary life. Professor Wilson Knight has pointed out[8] that "nature" is a principal theme in the play: the word itself is used in a variety of connotations, and the general notion is supported by animal imagery, by the centrality of the storm on the heath, and by Lear's stripping himself in symbolic rejection of the trappings of civilization. Professor A. C. Bradley,[9] again, has shown Shakespeare

---

[7] See Walter Clyde Curry, *Shakespeare's Philosophical Patterns* (Baton Rouge: Louisiana State University Press, 1937), pp. 83-84.

[8] *The Wheel of Fire*, pp. 197 f.

[9] *Shakespearean Tragedy*, pp. 271 f.

to have been especially concerned with religious beliefs in writing *Lear*. Almost every character voices a particular religious standpoint: Kent pins his faith to astrology; Edmund, the natural son, claims Nature as his goddess; even Cornwall's servants consider the moral government of the world; while Gloucester and Lear pass from stage to stage of religious experience, protected and sustained by Edgar's deep, if enigmatic, piety. Bradley, curiously enough, follows Swinburne in attaching great importance to the outburst of Gloucester:

> As flies to wanton boys, are we to the gods,
> They kill us for their sport.
>
> (IV. i. 38)

In his essay on "The Lear Universe," Professor Wilson Knight explains that, as the text clearly shows, this is only a passing phase in Gloucester's religious development;[10] it is, in fact, a temporary reaction of his superstitious nature to the fearful suffering he has had to endure. There is neither critical nor historical justification for treating this passage in isolation, as expressing the belief of Shakespeare himself. The Elizabethan so-called atheist denied orthodox views of revelation, but never approximated to the position of Thomas Hardy; to confer this unique distinction upon Shakespeare, in the face of all his other plays and of masses of contradictory evidence in *Lear* itself, was surely the crowning absurdity of naturalistic criticism. Shakespeare made in the image of a Victorian intellectual, is a sadly diminished and distorted figure. Bradley quotes Albany's

> This shows you are above,
> You justicers, that these our nether crimes
> So speedily can venge!
>
> (IV. ii. 78)

[10] *The Wheel of Fire*, p. 205.

but ignores his previous and much more significant exclamation:

> If that the heavens do not their visible spirits
> Send quickly down to tame these vile offences,
> It will come,
> Humanity must perforce prey on itself,
> Like monsters of the deep.[11]

(IV. ii. 46)

Divine intervention, he says, is necessary to control man's inordinate passions: an irregular line of three monosyllables introduces with particular solemnity the doom upon humanity left to itself. Taking this in conjunction with the stress upon religious attitudes generally, the varied uses of the word "nature" in the play, and the painful purgatory of Lear himself, may we not at least suspect Shakespeare of deliberately intending to present a world without revelation, in order to determine how far human nature could penetrate its mysteries and achieve religious and moral order apart from the gift of supernatural grace? *Macbeth* accepts the Christian dispensation, not just as historical setting, but as a philosophical structure integral to the dominant theme; *Othello* also, though less obviously, is built upon Christian values. It is unlikely that Shakespeare went momentarily pagan for the writing of *King Lear* (which is dated by Sir Edmund Chambers between *Othello* and *Macbeth*[12]) but more than likely that he should clinically isolate the pagan mind in order to work out a particular problem.

The pagan world in *King Lear* is presented with unusual care. Shakespeare has chosen an old story with its

---

[11] The significance of this passage was first pointed out to me by my former colleague, Professor D. G. James.

[12] *William Shakespeare: A Study of Facts and Problems* (2 vols., Oxford: Clarendon Press, 1930), I, 249.

roots far back in popular legend. Its incredible opening underlines the suggestion of antiquity, *Credo quia impossibile est* being the working principle of traditional story. The comparative informality of Lear's court; the suggestion of tracts of country, with no mention of any town; the stress on nature, animal imagery, and so forth, all support an atmosphere of primitive and pagan times. The gods are often called on, but God only once ("God's spies" (*King Lear*, V. iii. 17)), when Lear's purgatorial struggle is completed. More particularly, Lear swears "by Apollo" (I. i. 162), "by Jupiter" (II. iv. 21), and

> ...by the sacred radiance of the sun,
> The mysteries of Hecate, and the night;
> By all the operation of the orbs
> From whom we do exist, and cease to be. . . .
>> (I. i. 111)

"Hear, nature, hear; dear goddess, hear!" (I. iv. 297) he prays, and calls down the curse of sterility upon Goneril. His curses usually reflect a pagan nature-religion: "Blasts and fogs upon thee!" (I. iv. 321) and again:

> All the stored vengeances of heaven fall
> On her ingrateful top! Strike her young bones,
> You taking airs, with lameness!
>> (II. iv. 164)

He appeals to "the heavens" (II. iv. 274) for patience and placates the elements animistically: "I tax not you, you elements, with unkindness" (III. ii. 16).

In face of this careful suggestion of primitive antiquity and pagan thought, contemporary features are especially worthy of notice: they are not likely to be there by inadvertence. First there is "Poor Tom," the character assumed by Edgar in his flight. An Elizabethan audience would recognize the Tom o' Bedlam:

Poor Tom; that eats the swimming frog, the toad, the tad-
pole, the wall-newt and the water; that in the fury of his heart,
when the foul fiend rages, eats cow-dung for sallets, swallows
the old rat and the ditch-dog; drinks the green mantle of the
standing pool; who is whipped from tithing to tithing, and stock-
punished, and imprisoned.   (III. iv. 134)

These unfortunate creatures, mad and more than half
wild, roamed the common lands of Elizabethan England,
avoiding human company, except occasionally to beg or
to steal from an isolated farmstead. Driven from parish
to parish, under a Poor Law system which encouraged
every local authority to palm off its responsibilities upon
a neighboring community, the Tom o' Bedlam would be
seen by traveling merchants or companies of pleasure,
as he lurked behind hedgerows to avoid them, or if
hunger lent him courage, stood in the way to ask their
alms. Of all vagrants, he approached nearest the state
of savagery; and so Shakespeare utilizes such a figure
to suggest the unfamiliar through the familiar, the state
of primitive society through the contemporary savage of
whom his audience must at least have heard. Poor Tom
is possessed of devils with homely names: Smulkin, Hop-
dance, Flibbertigibbet; he sings snatches of old rhyme:

> S. Withold footed thrice the old;
> He met the night-mare, and her nine-fold;
>   Bid her alight,
>   And her troth plight,
> And, aroint thee, witch, aroint thee!   (III. iv. 125)

Shakespeare has filled his dialogue with the most intri-
guing references to folklore, so that Poor Tom is an invaluable addition to the primitive atmosphere. There is
especial subtlety in utilizing for this purpose a figure familiar in contemporary life, since not only is the notion

of the primitive given in this way a precisely recognized content, but also the fact that the remote gains its content only through a contemporary figure, serves to suggest a mutual relationship between past and present and, therefore, the relevance of King Lear's Britain to the England of Queen Elizabeth.

Among the many relevant meanings of "nature" in *King Lear*, two are of outstanding importance: first, nature as opposed to supernature, or the realm of grace; and secondly, nature as opposed to civilization. Nature without grace has its dignity, especially in the character of Edgar, but nevertheless, it is pitifully inadequate; the nature opposed to civilization, however, is clearer-eyed, nobler, as if civilization in itself were mere degeneracy. This latter use of the word implies Shakespeare's frequent theme of court *versus* country; in *As You Like It* and *The Winter's Tale*, for example, the simpler yet more significant life of the country is regarded as necessary to bring fresh vitality to an overcivilized court. The two themes of nature without grace and nature *versus* civilization combine contrapuntally in the purgation of Lear. Poor Tom is a concrete symbol of nature in both these senses and is so accepted by Lear from the first. Exposure to the storm has induced in the old king a new attitude to the suffering poor:

> Poor naked wretches, wheresoe'er you are,
> That bide the pelting of this pitiless storm,
> How shall your houseless heads and unfed sides,
> Your loop'd and window'd raggedness, defend you
> From seasons such as these? O, I have ta'en
> Too little care of this! Take physic, pomp;
> Expose thyself to feel what wretches feel,
> That thou mayst shake the superflux to them,
> And show the heavens more just.
>
> (III. iv. 28)

Feeling now his community with the poor, he must share their sufferings and distribute his surplus goods among them. This new thought has just come to him when the Fool rushes out, frightened, from the hovel where the disguised Edgar has been sheltering. Kent orders "Poor Tom" to come forth; and so Lear at the right moment is confronted by a specimen of the houseless poor, and one who, in the extremity of his apparent want, is an universal symbol, a concrete presentation of Lear's own thought. Poor Tom represents the extreme point of deprivation through which Lear must pass—loss of dignities, of wealth, of wits—in order to achieve his spiritual maturity. Lear himself quickly recognizes this: "Thou art the thing itself: unaccommodated man is no more but such a poor, bare, forked animal as thou art. Off, off, you lendings! come, unbutton here" (III. iv. 111). Discarding his clothes, he finally repudiates the civilized outlook, which sets false barriers between man and man: paradoxically, he has become clearer-headed in his madness. To an Elizabethan audience, it must surely have been significant that the figure which confirmed King Lear in this new wisdom, causing him to appreciate the purpose of suffering—the figure the old king refused to part from, calling him "learned Theban" (III. iv. 162), "noble philosopher" (III. iv. 177), and "good Athenian" (III. iv. 185)—was the poor, despised Tom o' Bedlam of their own experience. Here is the sharpest incongruity resolved, as in a metaphysical conceit of John Donne: the mystery of suffering laid bare to an ancient king by the contemporary village lunatic. It is a home-thrust like the parable of the Prodigal in modern dress, or like

> Christ walking on the water
> Not of Gennesareth, but Thames![13]

[13] Francis Thompson, *The Kingdom of God.*

Edmund is also a contemporary figure, this time a popular stage type, the Machiavel, and no doubt born out of Iago. He despises the superstitious credulity of his father: to blame the stars for our misfortunes is "the excellent foppery of the world" (I. ii. 128)—we might compare Iago's " 'tis in ourselves that we are thus or thus" (*Othello*, I. iii. 322). He is a natural son, and so takes Nature for his goddess. Pouring scorn on legitimacy and thrusting aside all "natural" feeling (another sense of the word) towards father and brother, he pursues his private ends, undeterred even by the disgusting cruelty of Cornwall and Regan to the aged Gloucester. He is pleasing to women, debonair, and with all the courtly graces. Shakespeare has distinguished his dialogue, which is mainly in prose, by a significant modernity of tone: "the excellent foppery of the world" is a phrase that, in *King Lear*, could only come from Edmund. His philosophy of unscrupulous egoism represents the usual stage version of Machiavelli: the Bastard in *King John* is an early attempt at such a character, of which Iago provides a deeper study, tracing this "enlightened selfishness" of the Renaissance to its diabolic source. Why, then, is Edmund admitted into the *Lear* world? Because in turning his back upon traditional morality, he appeals to nature as justifying this new freedom from moral restraint. Shakespeare, treating of mankind without a Savior, naturally requires a representative of the new paganism for comparison and contrast. Without the restraints of religion, Edmund exactly parallels the atrocious lives of Goneril and Regan, and is naturally drawn to make common cause with them. But there is contrast, also, between his clear cynicism and their attempts at self-excuse. Goneril and Regan have some color of complaint against their father, or at least persuade themselves that cause of complaint exists: he displays "the unruly waywardness that infirm and choleric years bring with them" (I. i. 301). Indeed, Goneril affects to complain, not of her father, but of his followers:

> Men so disorder'd, so debosh'd and bold,
> That this our court, infected with their manners,
> Shows like a riotous inn: epicurism and lust
> Make it more like a tavern or a brothel
> Than a graced palace.
>
> (I. iv. 263)

All she apparently requires is that he should "a little disquantity his train" (I. iv. 270), though we are in no doubt that she is pleased to be rid of him, when he rushes off impetuously to Regan. Regan's attitude is the same:

> For his particular, I'll receive him gladly,
> But not one follower.
>
> (II. iv. 295)

She, more than Goneril, tries to cover her evil purposes with a specious moralism:

> O, sir, to wilful men,
> The injuries that they themselves procure
> Must be their schoolmasters. Shut up your doors,
>
> (II. iv. 305)

she says, as the old man goes off again, angry and despairing, into the storm. Edmund, on the other hand, has no excuse in acting against "a credulous father and a brother noble" (I. ii. 195). His position is stated with aphoristic brevity: "All with me's meet that I can fashion fit" (I. ii. 200)—and this certainly suggests a deliberate, clear-eyed villainy more pernicious than the hot-blooded wickedness of Goneril and Regan. Shakespeare makes his Renaissance man reject, consciously and by an act of the rational will, a way of life which, though "foolish" (I. ii.

197), is recognized to be good; whilst the pagan cruelty of Goneril and Regan must be partially excused on the score of ignorance. It is significant that Edmund is the only character to be flippant with the gods: "Now, gods, stand up for bastards!" (I. ii. 22.) In him, then, Shakespeare takes a representative of the "new thought" and puts him back among his pagan kindred: he is again explaining the pagan world by reference to a familiar figure, and also implicitly criticizing the modern departure from traditional moral and religious standards. Oswald, similarly, is a typically overcivilized Renaissance courtier. When Edgar kills him, he speaks a broad rustic dialect for the occasion, though there is at the time no necessity in the plot for disguising his natural speech. The scene has been well taken by Professor Wilson Knight[14] to symbolize the overthrow of a false civilization by the steady rural virtues; it is the theme of court *versus* country, which is, of course, relevant to the central religious problem of *King Lear*, the problem of "nature."

One other instance of duality of time in *Lear* deserves mention. I have already shown how carefully the pagan atmosphere is built up and that Shakespeare generally refrains from reference to Christianity. There is a notable exception, however, in his treatment of Cordelia, who from first to last is associated with theological terminology and Christian symbol. The King of France will not believe her guilty of any monstrous offense:

> . . . which to *believe* of her [he says]
> Must be a *faith* that *reason* without *miracle*
> Could never plant in me.
>
> (I. i. 224)

A "Gentleman" later speaks of her to Kent, as shaking "The *holy water* from her *heavenly* eyes" (IV. iii. 32),

[14] *The Wheel of Fire*, p. 200.

when she read of her father's misfortunes. The reference is certainly to the holy water of ecclesiastical usage, which, being prepared with the addition of salt, furnishes an especially appropriate conceit. It is Cordelia who invokes

> All *blest* secrets,
> All you unpublish'd virtues of the earth,
>
> (IV. iv. 15)

bidding them "spring with her tears." Lear himself declares to her: "Thou art a soul in bliss . . . ," contrasting his own purgatorial state—"bound upon a wheel of fire" (IV. vii. 46)—in imagery clearly drawn from medieval religion. Most significant of all is a remark of the "Gentleman" who comes seeking the mad and wandering Lear (on the stage, at any rate, he would be the same gentleman who spoke to Kent):

> Thou hast one daughter,
> Who redeems nature from the general curse
> Which twain have brought her to.
>
> (IV. vi. 209)

It was Christ who redeemed nature from the general curse; and this passage reinforces a speech of France in the first scene of Act I, where also Cordelia seems to be compared with Our Lord:

> Fairest Cordelia, that art most rich, being poor;
> Most choice, forsaken; and most loved, despised!
>
> (I. i. 253)

On another occasion we find Cordelia herself using language which directly echoes a saying of Our Lord from St. Luke's Gospel:

> O dear father,
> It is thy business that I go about.[15]

[15] This passage was pointed out to me by one of my students, Mr. Cornelius Buckley.

(Cf. St. Luke 2:49: ". . . wist ye not that I must be about my Father's business?") Does this bold comparison suggest a poetic reason for her innocent yet ignominious death? In any event, it seems more than likely that, in this constant association of Cordelia with Christian doctrine, Shakespeare wished to suggest the foreshadowing of Christ in pure natures before His coming; as medieval thought looked back to Virgil, and as the Church has always regarded Moses and the prophets. However this may be, an atheistical Shakespeare would hardly have expressed his heroine in Christian terms. And Cordelia, whom Shakespeare has made "Christian"—or indeed Christlike—holds a position of central importance in the play, since she symbolizes the goal of Lear's purgatorial struggle. She is the good that he rejected in blind pride, and to which, in the new wisdom gained of suffering and sorrow, he was enabled to return, recognizing for the first time her true nature as "a soul in bliss." Moreover, these references from within the *Lear* world, recalling the contrasting world of Christian thought, demand of the audience an alert consciousness of both worlds and the tension existing between them. It is therefore quite evident that the paganism of *King Lear* is a deliberate reconstruction, planned for comparative appraisal in relation to the Christian world, and that it can in no wise be taken as Shakespeare's own interpretation of the universe as he saw it.

CHAPTER IV

THE TREATMENT OF CHARACTER (1)

MORE HAS been written about character than about any other theme in Shakespearean criticism. The study of character is, of course, important, though it is not everything; but the typical Victorian character criticism consisted entirely of psychological speculation and treated the text as providing scientific data rather than as mediating a poetic experience. By the end of the nineteenth century, Shakespearean criticism was almost limited to the discussion of characters, their motives, their self-consistency, and so forth; whilst treatment of the verse was usually confined to eulogies, in passing, of the appropriate anthological passages. Each critic refashioned Hamlet "after his own image,"[1] and wooed Rosalind or Imogen in frantically "poetic" prose. The reaction against this sort of thing has been very thorough, and modern writers are in no danger of confusing Shakespearean characters with real persons; but there is still some haziness about the principles governing Shakespeare's presentation of character.

Victorian criticism attempted to apply categories governing the naturalistic theater to a theater which was clearly not naturalistic. Naturalism aims at producing action and dialogue which resemble real life as closely as possible. An audience reacts to this type of play much as the "friend of the family" who, when things go wrong, is moved to sympathy, even though he is not personally

---

[1] For this dictum, cf. Bradbrook, *Elizabethan Stage Conditions*, p. 82.

involved in catastrophe. A naturalistic play actually affects the mind and the nerves precisely as they are affected by events in real life. As Miss Bradbrook says:

The modern playwright uses his technical resources to work directly on the nerves, and produce a state of bodily excitement. *The Emperor Jones* produces a powerful abdominal response, as much akin to literature as the feeling of going up in a lift.[2]

The only way to criticize characters in such a play is to regard them as one would acquaintances in real life, to take the dialogue as a direct guide to their states of mind, and to seek the motive of every action—in other words, to treat the play monistically, accepting the illusion of actuality and so regarding the play world as if it were the real world. Within limits, this is the reasonable approach to Ibsen, whose main concern, aside from certain propaganda purposes, was to present individual human beings upon the stage. Ibsen, it is said, lived with his characters: he knew their life history before the opening of his play, and could tell precisely how they would behave in any given circumstances. Few would have the hardihood to criticize Lyly or Chapman in a manner appropriate to Ibsen (which accounts for their undeserved neglect in the nineteenth century); but Shakespeare happened to possess, beyond his contemporaries, a sympathetic insight into human nature: his characters do not always conform to type, and sometimes surprise us by the "naturalness" of their behavior. Desdemona's "'Faith, half asleep" (*Othello*, IV. ii. 97) has already been mentioned.[3] There is also Rosalind, who faints when she sees the bloody napkin from Orlando's wound, and whose first words on coming round have a childlike and very natural pathos: "I would I were at home," she says (*As You Like It*, IV. iii. 162). Ophelia's restraint is equally surprising as she

[2] *Ibid.*, p. 125.   [3] See Chapter I, p. 9.

answers one of Hamlet's outbursts in the "nunnery" scene:

Ham.: You should not have believed me; for virtue cannot so inoculate our old stock but we shall relish of it: I loved you not.

Oph.: I was the more deceived![4]

(III. i. 118)

Again, Troilus, after a typically "metaphysical" consideration of Time, grows suddenly practical:

Cress.: Night hath been too brief.

Tro.: Beshrew the witch! with venomous wights she stays
     As tediously as hell, but flies the grasps of love
     With wings more momentary-swift than thought.
     You will catch cold, and curse me.

(*Troilus and Cressida*, IV. ii. 11)

This mingling of naturalism and conventionalism makes a further demand upon multiconsciousness, but the Victorian critics, culminating in Bradley, ignored Shakespeare's conventionalism and falsely simplified their approach by treating him as if he were a purely naturalistic writer. Yet in poetic drama, the verse form constitutes in itself a convention of fundamental importance, demanding a mode of attention quite different from that appropriate to naturalistic drama. Whereas naturalistic drama requires the same sort of attention as is given to happenings in ordinary life, poetic drama requires the same sort of attention as is necessary in reading lyric poetry. The impact of naturalistic drama on the mind is a crude and direct impact as of actual experience; but a situation in poetic drama can be appreciated only through a literary understanding of the poetry in which it is presented. The effect is not "abdominal," but is medi-

---

[4] Cf. Bradbrook, *Themes and Conventions of Elizabethan Tragedy*, p. 32.

ated by the intellect organically associated with a lively sensibility. The approach to poetic drama must, then, be fundamentally that of literary criticism. To treat the play world as if it were the real world, to apply to a play of Shakespeare the psychological categories applicable to actual life or to a play of Ibsen, must often result in serious misrepresentation. A naturalistic writer is able to reveal much about his characters in the way they speak: they are shown to be educated or uneducated, loquacious or taciturn, imaginative or practical. The writer of poetic drama may attempt something similar, though he works more by suggestion than imitation. Shakespeare imitates the "thick" speech of Hotspur[5] as directly as blank verse allows him. Later he suggests the contrast between Othello and Iago by contrasting the rhythm of their lines: unhurried, even, and dignified for Othello; flat, broken, and prosaic for Iago. Othello is given highly colored and exotic language ("antres vast and deserts idle" (I. iii. 140)), whilst in Iago imagery and reference are frequently to the physically unpleasant or the diabolical ("Horribly stuff'd with epithets of war" (I. i. 14); "Divinity of hell!" (II. iii. 356)). But direct imitation of speech characteristics is rare in Shakespeare, and even the oblique suggestion of character through the quality of verse is almost abandoned after *Othello*, since this method often requires verse inferior in subtlety and range to the writer's best. Critics have had a special tenderness for the "Othello music," probably because the Othello verse lacks subtlety and has an exaggerated strain of high romance, suggesting the weakness of his chivalric type.[6] A novelist such as John Dos Passos, who often

[5] So described by Lady Percy, in *II Henry IV*, II. iii. 24. For Shakespeare's imitation, see, for instance, *I Henry IV*, I. iii. 239 f.

[6] Dr. F. R. Leavis, "Diabolic Intellect and the Noble Hero," *Scrutiny*, VI (Dec., 1937), 259-283, suggests that the verse implies a habit of self-

writes in the first person, choosing as his mouthpiece a
simple-minded and uncultured "proletarian," similarly
denies himself the expression of his own more delicate
perceptions. After *Othello,* Shakespeare nearly always
gives his best verse to every character, regardless of individual differences; his dramatic material is thus completely transmuted into poetic terms. It is therefore dangerous to speak of certain characters as being more "poetic" than others; in poetic drama everyone necessarily
speaks poetry. On a naturalistic approach, we should
have to praise Macbeth's First Murderer for his refined
perception of the beautiful; his brief nightpiece being
justly celebrated:

> The west yet glimmers with some streaks of day:
> Now spurs the lated traveller apace
> To gain the timely inn.
>
> (III. iii. 5)

If the critic should insist on ascribing to the First Murderer a paradoxical strain of poetic feeling, there is, I
suppose, no logic which can finally prove him wrong; but
if he employs the same approach consistently throughout
even one play of Shakespeare, the resultant confusion will
be evidence enough of misdirected effort. Othello's eloquence has been much admired, although Othello himself assures us that he is the reverse of eloquent:

> Rude am I in my speech
> And little bless'd with the soft phrase of peace.
>
> (I. iii. 81)

This is not oratorical subtlety, like Antony's disclaimer:

> I am no orator, as Brutus is;
> But, as you know me all, a plain blunt man.
>
> (*Julius Caesar,* III. ii. 221)

---

dramatisation" in Othello. This is *psychologically* too subtle for Shakespeare, as should appear from the present chapter. Even had Shakespeare
reached such a conception he would have expressed it "directly" (see
pp. 81 f.).

And if we take it for sheer modesty, how are we to account for such accomplished oratory in one unused to the ways of polite society? Othello's ignorance of Venetian life, due to his foreign birth and constant absence at the wars, is a fact specially stressed in order to account for his being so readily deceived by Iago. Shakespeare would not intend this ingenuousness to be contradicted by a gift of eloquence; on the contrary, he would and does bring out Othello's unfamiliarity with civilized life by insisting on his rudeness of speech (to speak well was an essential social accomplishment in Elizabethan times). The quality of the Othello verse, including this characteristic eloquence, is, as I have said, an expression in poetic terms of Othello's nature. The eloquence is Shakespeare's, not Othello's, and we must accept the latter's statement at its face value: he is "rude in his speech." But in view of the convention of poetic drama this rudeness is not directly represented: Othello is articulate even in the statement of his own inarticulacy. His rudeness of speech and forthright nature are, however, obliquely suggested in the unwonted simplicity of the Othello verse.

When the element of conventionalism due to the fact that Shakespeare wrote his plays in verse, has been clearly recognized, it can be seen to involve an approach to character-presentation radically different from that of naturalism. Shakespeare makes little attempt directly to imitate ordinary speech, and we may not regard any psychological characteristic as necessarily implied in the formal properties of the dialogue. But further, how far is it possible to distinguish form and content? We do not think of the character, Macbeth, as a man who speaks in blank verse; we must not even think of him as a man of poetic imagination, since the poetry is Shakespeare's, not Macbeth's. What are we to say of imagery, which is manifestly "content" as well as "form"?   We cannot anachronistically claim Macbeth as a theatergoer on the strength of his "poor player" (V. v. 24), but Othello's "Pontic sea" (III. iii. 453) is surely chosen with some reference to the speaker's adventurous life. The matter is complicated, because there are undoubted elements of naturalism in Shakspeare: no rule of thumb is possible, but a sensitive reading will usually reveal the degree of conventionalism or naturalism in any particular speech. Beginning then from the conventionalism implied in the verse itself, we are forced to ask how far even the main notions conveyed by dialogue, and how far the action itself, may be taken as directly indicative of character. Is the naturalistic approach in any way valid for Shakespeare? The naturalistic approach treats stage characters as if they were real persons, and seeks a psychological explanation for their words and deeds. An audience in the naturalistic theater is busy with conjecture about the states of mind which would produce certain actions and remarks presented before them. But a Shakespearean audience is even more busy with the subtleties of a highly complex poetry, and it is unlikely that they would have time to spare for any but the most obvious naturalistic indications of character. There is no parallel here to the multi-consciousness of which I have spoken; the dual consciousness of play world and real world, or of past and present in an historical play, functions effortlessly on what is doubtfully termed the unconscious plane. To understand poetry, conscious effort is needed; and to penetrate character from dialogue and action, conscious effort is again needed, but of an entirely different type. It is thus a priori unlikely that naturalistic criticism should be very fruitful in dealing with Shakespeare. We must also remember Shakespeare's position in relation to the even more conventional miracle plays and interludes which preceded the Elizabethan drama; though, on the other side, we must take account of Renaissance influence and Shakespeare's own unusual insight into human nature. I have already suggested that we are dealing with a mixture of conventionalism and naturalism; neither approach can be wholly without value, but in the face of a strong naturalistic tradition in criticism, it is necessary to insist that naturalism must take second place.

First as to action: why does not Rosalind present herself to her father as soon as she discovers him in the Forest of Arden? "I met the duke yesterday and had much question with him [she says]: he asked me of what parentage I was; I told him, of as good as he; so he laughed and let me go" (*As You Like It*, III. iv. 38). Must we write her down as heartless and unfilial, despite her earlier outburst of grief at her father's long banishment? Shakespeare supplies no motive, but his own motive is plain enough: Rosalind is required to play Ganymede for some time longer, and all meetings of long-parted relatives must be left for the denouement in the Masque of Hymen. Any psychological explanation of Rosalind's behavior would introduce into her character a warring element foreign to the writer's intention. Why, again, does Edgar delay so long in revealing his true identity to the blind Gloucester? In a tragedy, questions of character are more important, and Edgar confesses his conduct as a fault:

> Never,—O fault!—reveal'd myself unto him,
> Until some half-hour past.
>
> (*King Lear*, V. iii. 192)

But he gives no explanation, doubtless because Shakespeare had no psychological explanation to hand. Edgar, having assumed the Poor Tom disguise, had become, for the deeper symbolic purposes of the play, a new, additional character, the Tom o' Bedlam. As such he had to guide the blinded Gloucester, furnishing a steady reminder of the ascetic principle; and though discarding his madness, he had to retain a rustic character for the overthrow of Oswald, which signifies the triumph of country over court. But for the meeting with Edmund, Edgar has resumed his own personality, though he appears, knightlike, with a flourish of trumpets, since the Renaissance man must be defeated by a representative of Christian chivalry. In the treatment of Edgar, propriety on the plane of naturalism yields to the needs of symbolical expression. Perhaps in the perfect plot we might expect a neat dovetailing of story and symbolic interpretation; but a perfect plot is too much to expect in union with the profoundly significant poetry of *King Lear*: Shakespeare would have no time to spare for precision of the detective-story kind. In most instances, however, psychological induction from the action is quite legitimate, so long as it is not pursued too far. When Malvolio flings down the ring before Viola-Cesario (*Twelfth Night*, II. ii), the incident is rightly taken to illustrate his "self-love," but it is probably not intended to imply an incipient jealousy over Olivia. The proper limits of such induction must be fixed by the reader's or audience's good sense.

In the matter of dialogue even greater care must be exercised. As an instance of false psychological induction Professor Schücking considers the notorious "I know you all" speech of Prince Henry.[7] Taken naturalistically, the speech suggests that Henry deliberately consorted with Falstaff and his crew, knowing them to be unworthy of

[7] *Op. cit.,* pp. 218 f.

his company, so that he might gain more approval by breaking with them than if he had never appeared to stand in need of reformation:

> *Prince:* I know you all, and will awhile uphold
> The unyoked humour of your idleness:
> Yet herein will I imitate the sun,
> Who doth permit the base contagious clouds
> To smother up his beauty from the world,
> That, when he please again to be himself,
> Being wanted, he may be more wonder'd at,
> By breaking through the foul and ugly mists
> Of vapours that did seem to strangle him.
> If all the year were playing holidays,
> To sport would be as tedious as to work:
> But when they seldom come, they wish'd for come,
> And nothing pleaseth but rare accidents.
> So, when this loose behaviour I throw off
> And pay the debt I never promised,
> By how much better than my word I am,
> By so much shall I falsify men's hopes;
> And like bright metal on a sullen ground,
> My reformation, glittering o'er my fault,
> Shall show more goodly and attract more eyes
> Than that which hath no foil to set it off.
> I'll so offend, to make offence a skill;
> Redeeming time when men think least I will.
>
> (*I Henry IV*, I. ii. 219)

On the naturalistic approach, one is shocked to note that Henry has apparently no affection for his boon companions; we should prefer genuine wild oats to such calculating and unprincely behavior. This interpretation, however, comes into conflict with every other indication of his character, excepting, for the sentimentalist, his final rejection of Falstaff. Considering the actual playhouse situation, we must remember that Shakespeare's task is an awkward one; his audience is patriotic, and he himself an ardent royalist, but he must present the hero of Agincourt in the dubious circumstances of his unregenerate youth. His purpose, surely, is to cast the glory of Agincourt back upon the shadows of Gadshill, to keep the prince hedged with divinity and unsmirched, even in the Boar's Head Tavern at Eastcheap. We must not take the speech naturalistically at all, so as to accuse Henry of a deliberate plan to secure favorable publicity. It is, rather, an objective statement of the facts, as they are, and as they will be (for it includes an element of the prophetic). Henry, we are told, even now understands the true nature of his companions: his judgment is unclouded, however he may take pleasure in low company; and we are next assured that we may enjoy the tavern scenes without impropriety, since Henry did, in fact, prove all the more popular for discarding his old associates on becoming king. The rejection of Falstaff is already anticipated, and we know that all will work out in accordance with the highest moral precepts. An audience used to speeches addressed directly to themselves, in which they are, as it were, taken into the confidence of a stage character, would understand Prince Henry's soliloquy in this way, as an objective statement of the facts; they would not think of it as implying this or that unfortunate blemish in his princely nature.

Professor Schücking has provided us with a key to the problem by drawing attention to the survival of "primitive" technique in Shakespeare. This is undoubtedly the right approach, although I object to the assumption that conventionalism is necessarily primitive and that a naturalistic presentation of character is the only truly dramatic method. We may, I think, best understand this older dramatic technique by regarding it as a blending of narrative with the "truly dramatic" or representational technique.   Medieval drama obviously unites the story-teller's art with a stylized version of ordinary speech and action; this is natural enough, since the miracle plays arose, not out of a scientific contemplation of human be-havior, but out of the literary forms and liturgical acts of Christian worship.   Pharaoh, in the Towneley cycle, announces himself as follows:

> Peas, of payn that no man pas;
> Bot kepe the course that I commaunde;
> And take good hede of hym that has
> Youre helth all holy in hys hande!
> For Kyng Pharro my fader was,
> And led thys lordshyp of thys land;
> I am hys hayre, as age wyll has,
> Ever in stede to styr or stand.
>
> All Egypt is myne awne
> To leede aftyr my law.
> I wold my myght were knawne
> And honoryd, as hyt awe, ...[9]

Pharaoh is speaking of himself precisely as one would write of him in the third person.   Again, Shakespeare more than once refers to the character of Herod, and, according to Professor Adams,[10] it is "almost certain" that he saw, as a boy, a performance of the Coventry cycle, in which the tyrant Herod figures prominently.   Herod, like Ercles, was "a part to tear a cat in" *(A Midsummer Night's Dream*, I. ii. 31), and it is interesting to note that the character objectively describes his own "rag-ing," while he is in process of enacting it.   On learning that the Wise Men have gone home another way, he cries:

---

[9] Quoted from Adams (ed.), *op. cit.*, p. 125.   [10] *Ibid.*, p. 158 n.

A-nothur wey? owt! owt! owtt!
Hath those fawls traytvrs done me this ded?
I stampe! I stare! I loke all abowtt!
Myght I them take, I schuld them bren at a glede!
I rent! I rawe! and now run I wode![11]

Shakespeare is never so "primitive" as this, though he is undoubtedly nearer the conventionalism of the medieval miracles than he is to the naturalism of Ibsen. With Pharaoh's speech we may compare the opening soliloquy of *Richard III*:

> . . . since I cannot prove a lover,
> To entertain these fair well-spoken days,
> I am determined to prove a villain
> And hate the idle pleasures of these days.
> Plots have I laid, inductions dangerous,
> By drunken prophecies, libels and dreams,
> To set my brother Clarence and the king
> In deadly hate the one against the other:
> And if King Edward be as true and just
> As I am subtle, false and treacherous,
> This day should Clarence closely be mew'd up,
> About a prophecy. . . .
>
> (I. i. 28)

Gloucester speaks of himself dispassionately, like an on-looker. No one actually "determines to prove a villain" or estimates himself as "subtle, false, and treacherous"; at least such a character would be very rare, much rarer than they appear in Shakespeare. There is no exact Shakespearean parallel to Herod's speech, since Shakespeare is more naturalistic—and more economical—than the writers of miracles: he does not need to give in the dialogue an account of what is being adequately portrayed in action. But much less can be expressed in action on the

[11] *Ibid.*, p. 163.

Elizabethan stage than on the modern, naturalistic stage, and the narrative mode is used a good deal—always, of course, blended with the dramatic. Naturalistic expression of physical and mental states must have been limited by the stylization demanded by verse-speaking and the unrealistic settings: the audience is therefore directly informed, in a brief phrase, of conditions which a modern actor would convey entirely without words. Hermia's "I swoon almost with fear" (*A Midsummer Night's Dream*, II. ii. 154) and Lear's "My wits begin to turn" (*King Lear*, III. ii. 67) are not expressions which would occur naturally to people placed in their respective situations; but they are just what an indifferent observer, or a novelist, might record of them. This method of partial narrative is appropriate to poetic drama, since it renders the psychological situation clear without transferring attention from the verse to the processes of naturalistic induction. Moreover, verse and narrative were born together in the remotest ages, and it is natural to find a narrative flavor in verse drama; the drama which directly imitates real life grew out of a scientific temper distrustful of the poetic imagination. No poet could allow Romeo his last kiss and a silent death; however absurd it may be for Romeo to speak at such a time, the poet must put this crucial situation into words: "Thus with a kiss I die" (*Romeo and Juliet*, V. iii. 120). The Shakespearean character may be thought of as telling his own story, with appropriate gesture and movement, from a standpoint well outside himself; though there are sudden irruptions of naturalism which demand rapid adjustment on the part of the audience. This narrative method explains our First Murderer's night piece. In the absence of scenery and lighting, atmosphere had to be obtained entirely through the poetry, and Shakespeare did

not much mind who spoke his descriptive speeches. The
matter-of-fact Horatio has a lyrical outburst upon the
dawn:

> But, look, the morn in russet mantle clad,
> Walks o'er the dew of yon high eastward hill,
>   (*Hamlet*, I. i. 166)

and the usually gruff Enobarbus is selected for that
tremendous description of Cleopatra "upon the river of
Cydnus" (*Antony and Cleopatra*, II. ii. 192):

> The barge she sat in, like a burnished throne,
> Burn'd on the water. . . .
>   (II. ii. 196)

No one has put down Banquo for a bird fancier on the
strength of his "temple-haunting martlet" (*Macbeth*, I.
vi. 4), and it would be dangerous to endow Horatio with
an artist's vision. The question of Enobarbus is more
complicated, since he did die in suspicious circumstances,
of a broken heart; but that was induced by the generosity
of Antony, not by any relenting in his attitude to Cleopatra. As Antony's henchman, however, he was the only
probable witness of the Cydnus affair, and so the obvious
person to describe it; if there be any deeper psychological
propriety in allotting the speech to him, I should imagine
it to be purely coincidental.

Consideration of the "narrative element" in Shakespeare may seem thus far only to have further confounded
a sufficiently complicated situation. There are admittedly
speeches and parts of speeches which must be interpreted
psychologically, by the naturalistic method: Desdemona's
"'Faith, half asleep," etc. And there are also speeches
and parts of speeches, which, treated in the same way,
yield a nonsensical result, because they are intended as
objective statements, not directly to be ascribed to the

characters who deliver them. But the approach to character, initially complicated by the fact that Shakespeare
wrote in verse, has nevertheless been considerably simplified for us by his employment of the narrative method. It
is clearly impossible, in poetic drama, to convey character
adequately by naturalistic means: so much is to be ascribed
directly to the writer rather than the character. Moreover, as we have said, an audience attending to poetry cannot be expected to pursue the subtle implications of character, which may lurk in a casual phrase. Shakespeare and
other dramatists in the popular tradition solve the problem, no doubt quite unconsciously, by presenting us with
an authentic outline of each important character, clearly
stated either by himself or by another. Thus Gloucester's speech, already quoted, sums up his nature for us
with unusual clarity; and Malvolio's fatal flaw is revealed by Olivia at his first appearance: "O, you are sick
of self-love, Malvolio, and taste with a distempered
appetite" (*Twelfth Night*, I. v. 97). Conventionalism
and naturalism are blended in various proportions for
this direct presentation of character. Gloucester's "I
am determined to prove a villain" could never be
seriously spoken by mortal man, whereas we may well
regard Olivia's timely rebuke as a good example of
her insight into character. But bearing in mind Shakespeare's general practice, it is significant that it is on
Malvolio's first appearance that Olivia speaks so remarkably apropos; the dramatist's main concern at the
time is surely with Malvolio and not with Olivia. It is
doubtful, then, whether we are justified in speaking of
Olivia's shrewdness in this connection; and it is quite certain that we should not take "self-revelations" like the
Gloucester speech as implying an exceptional degree of

self-awareness either in Shakespeare's characters or, more generally, in the Renaissance mind. The Macbeth soliloquies provide a more difficult case in point. Macbeth's is hardly the career of an introvert, and there is no real need to interpret his soliloquies as elaborate self-analysis. It is merely that, through him, Shakespeare makes explicit the general psychology of crime, by means not wholly unlike the "expressionism" of today. For instance, in an aside after the witches' first "two truths" have been established, and Macbeth has been proclaimed both Glamis and Cawdor, he says:

> Present fears
> Are less than horrible imaginings:
> My thought, whose murder yet is but fantastical,
> Shakes so my single state of man that function
> Is smother'd in surmise, and nothing is
> But what is not.
>
> (I. iii. 137)

Taking this naturalistically, we should have to say that Macbeth is carefully examining himself, defining the precise nature of his own mental disturbance. What I suggest is that Macbeth was indeed divided in mind; its simple state was shaken; but he was not thinking about his mind: he was thinking about Duncan and about himself as king. In a naturalistic drama, he would show abstraction and some confusion, and might mutter a half-formed phrase about the witches' prophecy or his own hopes and fears. But Shakespeare presents coherently and in fully articulate poetry what is conscious but not self-conscious in Macbeth. The articulateness is Shakespeare's, and does not issue from any unusual self-awareness on Macbeth's part. Similarly, the "To-morrow and to-morrow" soliloquy expresses, in Shakespeare's terms, the hopelessness of a hardened sinner, to whom the universe has now no meaning. The statement preceding it is quite objective:

> I have almost forgot the taste of fears:
> The time has been, my senses would have cool'd
> To hear a night-shriek; and my fell of hair
> Would at a dismal treatise rouse and stir
> As life were in't: I have supp'd full with horrors;
> Direness, familiar to my slaughterous thoughts,
> Cannot once start me.
>
> (V. v. 9)

A novelist would write in such terms about his villain, but no villain would refer objectively to his own slaughterous thoughts; and no one so insensitive would be alert to his own insensitivity. The blending of narrative with "purely dramatic" method enables Shakespeare to present characters much more clearly than is possible with a naturalistic technique. In a naturalistic drama the audience is so often left to make what it can of a gesture, a grimace, and a few incoherent phrases. We live in an age both incoherent and evasive: people cannot speak out and would not if they could: it is the last age to attempt a naturalistic, purely imitative drama. Expressionism is one way—not a beautiful way—out of an impasse which would never have been created but for the interfering "logic" of neoclassical and naturalistic criticism. For in Shakespearean dialogue, character is not obscurely hinted at, as in the conversations of real life, but expressed by direct statement, with an intellectual and emotional precision only possible to great poetry.

Professor Schücking tries to systematize Shakespeare's procedure in the presentation of character and lays down a number of rules, which, however, he cannot always claim as infallible. In general, whatever a character tells us of himself, or of another character, we are to believe, unless there is some obvious reason for not doing so; particularly, the first time a principal character is introduced, either personally or in the dialogue of another, we are to take what is said of him as objectively true; and we are not to take such statements psychologically, as implying a high degree of self-awareness, etc.[12] Heroes will speak of their own good qualities, and villains be aware of their own villainy and of the heroes' virtues; but we must not regard the heroes as self-conceited or the villains as unduly cynical. This approach is generally much more fruitful than the psychological approach of Professor Bradley; but Shakespeare did not work to rule—his dramatic methods were modifications *ad hoc* of a living tradition. Shakespeare's is a mixed mode, and there is no substitute for critical good sense in deciding the pros and cons of each particular problem. Was Macbeth really

> ...too full o' the milk of human kindness
>   To catch the nearest way,
>
> *(Macbeth, I. v. 18)*

or is this merely his wife's mistaken judgment?[13] Macbeth himself, debating the murder, seems to be deterred only by fear of the consequences. Perhaps Shakespeare has been inconsistent; or perhaps he intends Lady Macbeth to be mistaken; or, again, Macbeth may have certain scruples on the score of "human kindness," which he represents to himself as merely prudential—he may not know himself as well as his wife knows him. Unless Shakespeare has made a mistake, then, we can only resolve this difficulty by combining the naturalistic approach with the conventional. Again, Othello is first introduced

---

[12] I have tried here to summarize Professor Schücking's general thesis—I hope without serious misrepresentation.

[13] The question is discussed by Schücking, who decides characteristically that Shakespeare has been inconsistent (*op. cit.*, pp. 70 f.).

to us through Iago's opening speech, yet we cannot accept Iago's unflattering portrait of him, at least without qualification. There may, indeed, be more in it than orthodox criticism has allowed: Othello perhaps did "love his own pride and purposes" (I. i. 12); and at times, particularly in his speech "Farewell the plumed troop," etc. (III. iii. 349), we may feel the aptness of Iago's phrase:

> . . . a bombast circumstance
> Horribly stuff'd with epithets of war.
>
> (I. i. 13)

The Iago portrait, nevertheless, is highly impressionistic and probably tells us more about Iago than Othello; it is emphatically not the simple statement of truth which we should expect in a first reference to the hero. But since Iago's own nature is made abundantly clear in the same speech, the audience would naturally be chary of accepting his word about Othello: there is little danger of confusion in this recourse to a relatively naturalistic presentation.[14]

Professor Schücking regards the self-knowledge of Iago and Edmund as purely conventional, but I should question this assumption. Both are of the Machiavel type, characters illustrating the new Renaissance cynicism, and it is therefore consistent to regard them as being cynically self-aware. Their soliloquies have a gusto very different from Gloucester's objective precision. Each of them recognizes not only his own villainy, but the virtues of those he is plotting against; yet I cannot consider this as a conventional recognition, since the virtues are recognized only to be despised:

> The Moor is of a free and open nature,
> That thinks men honest that but seem to be so,

[14] So Schücking, who apparently sees no truth at all in this characterization of Othello (*op. cit.*, p. 66).

And will as tenderly be led by the nose
As asses are.

(I. iii. 405)

Similarly Edmund speaks of

A credulous father! and a brother noble,
Whose nature is so far from doing harms,
That he suspects none; on whose foolish honesty
My practices ride easy!

(*King Lear*, I. ii. 195)

In contrast, Shakespeare makes only a slight attempt to give naturalistic color to Oliver's recognition of Orlando's superiority to himself:

I hope I shall see an end of him; for my soul, yet I know not why, hates nothing more than he. Yet he's gentle, never schooled and yet learned, full of noble device, of all sorts enchantingly beloved, and indeed so much in the heart of the world, and especially of my own people, who best know him, that I am altogether misprised.

(*As You Like It*, I. i. 170)

A real-life Oliver would be more inclined to accuse Orlando of assuming a false benevolence for the express purpose of ousting him from the affections of his people. There is, however, less naturalism in the comedies than in the tragedies, where character is more important.

Character can, of course, be presented only in outline by the method of direct statement: the brisk summaries which characters give of themselves and of one another resemble, and are probably akin to, the Theophrastan character sketch, which was growing popular in Shakespeare's day. Maria's description of Malvolio ("The devil a puritan that he is," etc. (*Twelfth Night*, II. iii. 159)) reads not unlike a lighter version of, say, the seventeenth-century Bishop Earle. How far, then, may we look for indications of character, apart from this conventional "narrative" method of direct statement? Shakespeare, as we have seen, mingled naturalistic expression of character with the conventional, and it is therefore impossible to prescribe exact limits to the naturalistic approach. Shakespearean drama is not a parlor game but art that has grown out of life. The critic has no rules, only a delicate sense of verbal implications. Obvious naturalistic inductions are, of course, valid: the dialogue of Falstaff reflects one personality; the dialogue of Lear another and very different personality.   In outline a character will usually correspond to the account given of him by the method of direct statement: Malvolio's "self-love," pointed out at first by Olivia, dominates his dialogue and action throughout the play. He is a recognizable stage type; and we are safest in limiting naturalistic induction generally to the recognition of such types. Most of the subtle psychological problems raised by Shakespearean critics were probably never considered by Shakespeare himself. If they had been he would have solved them for us; but they have been created *ex nihilo* by his own indifference and the perverseness of critical activity. Shakespeare's characters are not psychologically treated in any modern sense; he is not concerned with minute individual differences or with the genesis, in a remote past, of this or that characteristic. He does not explore the "subconscious"; his concern, as a practical dramatist, is mainly with the stage types held as common property among Elizabethan writers: Jaques, the melancholy man; Sir Andrew, the "natural"; Parolles, the cowardly braggart. The only psychology consciously applied in Shakespeare is that advocated by Ben Jonson, which differentiates human types according to their "humors" (passions or, perhaps, attitudes); but the humor psychology itself is never taken quite seriously, and popular use of the word "humor" (like our own addiction to the "complex") is unmercifully ridiculed in *Henry V* and in *The Merry Wives of Windsor*. Even commonplaces of the modern dramatists' treatment of character are strangely neglected: Lear, Macbeth, Antony, and Cleopatra change considerably in the course of a play, but development or retrogression of this sort is rare; there is little influence of one character upon another; and there is frequently a shameless disregard of motive. Professor Schücking has suggested that a character may change, not by psychological development, but quite arbitrarily for dramatic convenience, from scene to scene. I believe this to be true of the comedies, but in tragedy, where considerations of character are more important, Shakespeare's consistency can, I think, usually be vindicated.[15] Professor Stoll, in *Art and Artifice in Shakespeare*, goes so far as to deny altogether the relevance of psychology to Shakespeare's treatment of character. To him, the tragic heroes themselves present combinations of self-contradictory qualities which could not coexist in an actual person. Othello is incapable of jealousy, yet falls into a jealous rage, which, however, he in some way transcends; Macbeth is a hero who commits murder and yet remains a hero—remains, as it were, outside the deed he has committed. To accept such a view would render criticism nugatory and impoverish the function of drama. One could only regard poetic drama, in such circumstances, as the calling up of patterned emotional responses without any objective intellectual content: its function would be the same as a symphony in music. It is significant that Professor Stoll does make use of musical parallels; and also that he shows a strong regard for the precepts of Aristotle's

---

[15] Exceptions are considered in the next chapter.

Poetics. Had Shakespeare deferred to Aristotle, Macbeth would have remained a hero throughout. Shakespeare, however, was not concerned with the nature of tragedy, but with the nature of sin, and it is the nature of sin to harden heroes into villains, crime by crime. Shakespeare's characters, we know, are not photographic transcripts of human individuals; but neither are they monsters, inconsistent with humanity as we know it. They are, as it were, abstracted from humanity, yet functionally related to it: types and humors—even allegorical and symbolic figures, as I shall afterwards show.[16] A type presents in abstract certain features common to a class; a humor is a human being reduced to a dominant principle; an allegorical figure personalizes an abstraction; a symbol stands for a greater reality, human or divine: all are simplifications of the actual, and are simplified to take their place in an interpretation of experience.

Shakespeare's technique of character presentation is not merely the result of theatrical exigencies; it accurately reflects his own, and the Elizabethan, mode of thought. He is concerned for a number of things besides character: ideas, words, wit. His speeches do not merely illustrate their speakers: what is said is more important than why it should be said. A joke is there for the joke's sake, and a wise word for its wisdom. In a way, he is more natural than the naturalists. In ordinary conversation we ought, I suppose, to be able to trace every remark of our companion to its psychological source, to see it as reflecting his pride, or humility, or the fact that he was kicked by a horse in infancy. But in point of fact, most of us are content most of the time to be interested in what is said, for its own sake. The naturalistic playwright, however, is deliberately revealing

[16] See Chapter V, pp. 117 ff.

character all the time; his interest in character has become morbid; whereas Shakespeare, especially in the comedies, must have written his brilliant dialogue with little thought of why this particular subject should be given to this particular character; introducing the subjects he himself wanted to write about, and avoiding the obviously inappropriate by an unconscious but unfailing tact. In the matter of character itself, he is not interested in the details of individual behavior, in the minor differences which separate man from man; his interest is general and philosophical. In his comedies he is concerned with "designs for living"; hence the importance of the type: his tragedies are even more metaphysical, treating generally of man in his relation to the universe and to God. His themes are the broad themes of humanity: birth, marriage, and death; sin and amendment, joy and sorrow. This is well known, and he is therefore described as "universal"; but it is not usually recognized that in devoting himself to these large matters, he generally neglects those questions of individual psychology dear to the modern mind. *Macbeth* traces the gradual hardening of a sinner, as he sinks deeper and deeper into crime, losing his grasp of metaphysical reality, to end in the atrophy of faith. The plan is medieval, in accordance with the ethical teaching of St. Thomas Aquinas.[17] There is no attempt to account for Macbeth's behavior in terms of his earlier life; we do not hear that he was ill-treated by his nurse or bullied by a senior officer at the beginning of his army career. Such factors of individual case history, and the deterministic suggestion that goes with them, are peculiar to the naturalistic drama, which has developed in a period of religious skepticism and scientific superstition. What a promising triangle Shakespeare overlooked in *Romeo and Juliet!* After one sight of

[17] Curry, *op. cit.*, Chapter IV, "Macbeth's Changing Character."

Juliet, Romeo thinks of Rosaline no more; he is not interested in the comparison of his new love with the old, nor is Shakespeare interested in those heart-searchings which, conscientiously exploited, would fill a ten-and-sixpenny novel today. Romeo and Juliet are *"star-crossed lovers"*: the concern is metaphysical—for romantic love and its place in the universe; and the play raises questions which are not fully answered until *Antony and Cleopatra* and the late romances. Even *Lear* is more like a poetic treatise in mystical theology than a "portrait" by one of our psychological novelists. We know nothing of Lear's private tastes, except his hunting, which serves to suggest the old man's terrifying vitality. It does not occur to us to wonder what he likes for dinner or to speculate upon his choice of books; no one has seen in his echoes of Horace[18] an anachronistic devotion to the Classics. Nor is there any suggestion that his late wife was responsible for Lear's uncertain temper and possessive attitude towards his daughters. What we are shown is the gradual enlightening of spiritual blindness. Lear's hasty temper and unwisdom co-operate with the evil outside himself to denude him of dignities, of self-respect, even of sanity. But in the depths—in what a mystic would term "the dark night of his soul"—he gains, through deprivation, a new insight into his own real nature as a man, and into his relationship with the universe. This mysterious process of purgatorial cleansing, of renewal by negation, is not presented in the details of an individual character. As Lear unbuttons and casts off his lendings, so Shakespeare strips him of the accidents of personality, so that only universal humanity remains. Shakespeare's interest is in man rather than

---

[18] See Edmund Blunden, "Shakespeare's Significances," reprinted in *Shakespearean Criticism, 1919-1935*, ed. Anne Bradby (World's Classics; London: Oxford University Press, 1936).

men; he is medieval in his concentration on those factors which men have in common, rather than the individualizing factors which keep them apart.

The mixed mode of character presentation favored by Shakespeare and the popular dramatic tradition depends for its validity upon the principle of multiconsciousness. It is only when the play world is recognized as distinct from the real world, that the conventions of direct statement may function without ambiguity, and the audience impose upon itself a limit to the exploration of character through dialogue. Naturalism, on the other hand, with its monistic attitude to dramatic illusion, can admit only the minimum of convention necessary to any stage performance. The change from conventionalism to naturalism, from multiconsciousness to what we might call theatrical monism, reflects not only a change in technical resources but also a profound change in metaphysical outlook. Theatrical naturalism, as we have seen, is a product of philosophical materialism, which monistically denies reality to the supernatural. Scientific interest in individual case history, as displayed by Ibsen and the naturalists, is the only sort of interest in humanity possible when humanity has been ousted from its central position in the universe. But the Shakespearean presentation of character depends on a multiconsciousness related to that balance of opposites which constitutes the universe of Christianity: God and man; spirit and matter; time and eternity. Vestiges of this multiconsciousness remaining today still influence presentation of character on the popular stage and in the films. The motion picture rarely attempts psychological dissection, since its technique demands action and constantly changing scenes. Character types can usually be labeled without difficulty, and they change within a film only in very obvious ways: rising superior to, or sinking under, some particular vice; growing harsher or more tender in the course of time, etc. For these purposes, a few short scenes representing "turning points" or "critical junctures" must suffice. Love at first sight and sudden conversions are as common in the films as in Shakespearean comedy. In each they are "conventions"; we do not expect that sort of behavior to be so frequent in actual life as upon the stage. They are, of course, necessary for technical reasons, since psychological detail is possible only in a play of few characters and little action. But practical necessity does not explain the prevalence of such illogical occurrences in the world's most popular stories; sudden love, sudden hate, sudden conversion, are the staple material of fiction from folk tale to parish monthly. The popular mind is apparently convinced that there are limits to human self-determination, and that forces exist outside man, which may act upon him for good or evil. Folk legend lies beyond the neat categories of psychological motivation, in a world of signs and portents, of mysterious promptings, in which the supernatural plays a guiding and controlling part; and Shakespeare's world is the world of folk legend more profoundly understood—a development, in fact, of medieval Christianity. Shakespeare's unpsychological treatment of character, including his notoriously uncertain motivation, suggests the existence of a guiding and controlling Power beyond the human will. Viola commits her problems to a development, the arbitration of Time:

> O time! thou must untangle this, not I,
> It is too hard a knot for me to untie!
> *(Twelfth Night,* II. ii. 41)

whilst to Malvolio "all is fortune" (II. v. 27). "Time" and "fortune" both mean Providence. Hamlet's delay is purposive at last, as he waits on God;

Our indiscretion sometimes serves us well,
When our deep plots do pall: and that should teach us
There's a divinity that shapes our ends,
Rough-hew them how we will.

(Hamlet, V. ii. 8)

And at the end of Shakespeare's career we see, in Prospero, divinity itself shaping human ends, that good may come out of ill. So the philosophic Gonzalo exclaims:

Was Milan thrust from Milan, that his issue
Should become kings of Naples? O, rejoice
Beyond a common joy, and set it down
With gold on lasting pillars: In one voyage
Did Claribel her husband find at Tunis
And Ferdinand, her brother, found a wife
Where he himself was lost, Prospero his dukedom
In a poor isle and all of us ourselves
When no man was his own.

(The Tempest, V. i. 205)

The intimate tie between human destiny and the significance of the universal order is central to Shakespeare's thought, as to medieval Christianity. It is also the core of tragedy, since human beings have no dignity in themselves but only in virtue of their central place in an universal plan. Despite a plethora of critical formulas, the Augustans were unable to produce a single tragedy worth comparing with even the smallest of Elizabethan fry. For the prevalent deistic rationalism, it was impossible to think of the supernatural as impinging on the natural from outside, so as to alter the the course of natural events: God had retreated to the position of *primum mobile*, and Heaven, no longer concerned in the affairs of men, had ceased to "peep through the blanket of the dark" (*Macbeth*, I. v. 54). Even Samuel Johnson, that great churchman, was stirred to risibility at the "blanket" metaphor. "Low words" such as "peep" and "blanket" were deemed inappropriate to the dignity of Heaven—which indicates that the idea of heaven might be somewhat insecure. As heaven grew inaccessible, man shrank in importance, and having lost his humility with his unique destiny, plumed himself on the infallibility of his social poise, which is exemplified in the dubious values of Restoration and eighteenth-century comedy. Neoclassicism next gave way to naturalism; the last citadel of human dignity fell before the march of mind; and man became "a poor, bare, forked animal" indeed (*King Lear*, III. iv. 112), though with a complicated prenatal history. Only the popular mind, as revealed in the popular theater, preserved in crude melodrama something of the ancient wonder and a sense that man is not in himself an adequate cause of his own remarkable history. On this, if on anything, the future of the drama—as of any social decency—must ultimately depend.

CHAPTER V

THE TREATMENT OF CHARACTER (II)

SPECIFIC applications of the principle of multiconsciousness serve to explain certain particular conventions governing Shakespeare's presentation of character. In this chapter I propose to consider the most important of these conventions one by one.

Direct Address

It is not unusual, in pre-Shakespearean drama, for a character to address himself directly to the audience. Nicholas Udall's *Roister Doister*, probably written while he was headmaster of Eton (1534-41),[1] opens with Mathewe Merygreeke alone on the stage. Addressing the audience directly, he gives an account of himself and of Rafe Roister Doister, which lasts for sixty-four lines. Then Rafe enters in search of Mathewe, and we have an interesting example of the mixture of "narrative" with the "truly dramatic" mode: in the first eleven lines there is only one line of "natural" dialogue, in which Rafe addresses Mathewe; for the rest, Rafe is speaking his thoughts aloud, quite unnaturalistically, and Mathewe is still addressing the audience:

> *R. Royster:* Come, death, when thou wilt! I am weary of my life!
> *M. Mery:* I told you, I, we should wowe another wife!
> *R. Royster:* Why did God make me suche a goodly person?
> *M. Mery:* He is in by the weke. We shall haue sport anon.
> *R. Royster:* And where is my trustie friende, Mathew Merygreeke?

[1] So Adams (ed.), *op. cit.*, p. 423 n.

> *M. Mery:* I wyll make as I sawe him not.
> He doth me seeke.
> *R. Royster:* I haue hym espyed, me thinketh,
> yond is hee.
> Hough, Mathew Merygreeke, my friend!
> a worde with thee!
> *M. Mery:* I wyll not heare him, but make as I
> had haste.
> (Pretending to go)
> Farewell, all my good friendes! the tyme
> away dothe waste;
> And the tide, they say, tarieth for no man![2]

There is nothing in Shakespeare quite parallel to this, but his essential continuity with the earlier drama is demonstrated in an occasional passage. Launce, in *The Two Gentlemen of Verona,* has a long monologue during which he addresses himself directly to the audience and describes his leaving home, with clownish illustrations: "Nay, I'll show you the manner of it. This shoe is my father . . ." (II. iii. 15). Much later in Shakespeare's career, there is the notorious example of the Fool in *King Lear.* When the others have taken shelter from the storm, at the end of Act III, scene ii, he turns to the audience before following them, and delivers a curious parting speech:

> This is a brave night to cool a courtezan.
> I'll speak a prophecy ere I go:
> When priests are more in word than matter;
> When brewers mar their malt with water;
> When nobles are their tailors' tutors;
> No heretics burn'd, but wenches' suitors;
> When every case in law is right;
> No squire in debt, nor no poor knight;

---

[2] Actus I, scaena ii. ll. 1 f., in *ibid.,* p. 426.

When slanders do not live in tongues;
Nor cutpurses come not to throngs;
When usurers tell their gold i' the field;
And bawds and whores do churches build;
Then shall the realm of Albion
Come to great confusion:
Then comes the time, who lives to see 't,
That going shall be used with feet.
This prophecy Merlin shall make; for I live before his time.

(III. ii. 79)

The passage is usually regarded as a non-Shakespearean insertion into the text, perhaps an *ad hoc* invention of the actor who played the Fool. It is, however, not without trenchancy and bears a relevance to the deeper themes of the play unlikely to be attained in a casual, catchpenny interpolation. There is, of course, "confusion" in the prophecy; its first three lines describe an undesirable state of affairs; judgment upon the fourth line might vary with opinion; lines 5 to 9 are utopian; and line 10 is ambiguous, since we are uncertain whether the "bawds and whores" are now converted, or whether their church building may mask less laudable activities. An impotent conclusion reminds us of the futility of seeking any wholly intelligible paraphrase. But the references to religion, to the disturbed social order (l. 3), to the distribution of wealth, and to sexual sin, are significant, since these very themes are of major importance in the play itself. Under a cloak of nonsense, the prophecy collects a number of the *Lear* themes in the form of a popular broadside and with contemporary application; as if Shakespeare wished here to underline the relevance of the *Lear* world to contemporary affairs. The Fool's last piece of glorious nonsense is a complicated manipulation of the time theme, always a favorite subject of

Shakespeare's poetic speculation; it focuses attention upon the duality of time-reference, which is so important to an understanding of the play:[3] "This prophecy Merlin shall make; for I live before his time." Direct address to the audience shatters all possibility of dramatic illusion, in order to make clear the need for alert cross reference between ancient and contemporary Britain. The quality of the verse is no argument against Shakespearean authorship: the style is deliberately simplified and pedestrian, not unlike that of the Epilogue to *The Tempest*. The intention, no doubt, is to parody the broadside manner;[4] but the lines are not doggerel, and a suggestion of speech rhythm, preserved by variety of stress, indicates the work of an accomplished writer of verse.

If the passage be genuine, it is interesting to find Shakespeare employing direct address at the height of his powers. The convention can be acceptable only to an audience conscious simultaneously of play world and real world. The Fool is recognized as stepping out of the story for a moment: he addresses the audience in character as the Fool, but not in any direct reference to the story. This half-and-half adjustment is rendered possible by the fact that the audience recognize him (a) as actor belonging to their own (real) world, and (b) as character, belonging to the play world. Launce's speech implies an even bolder conventionalism. The Fool's prophecy concerned matters common to the Lear story and contemporary life, occupying a no-man's-land between the play world and the real world; but Launce takes the audience into his confidence about events which

[3] See Chapter III, pp. 57 f.
[4] Cf. Arden edition, p. 129 n. Here it is suggested that the passage "may almost be called a parody of some lines, called 'Chaucer's Prophecy'"—a pseudo-Chaucerian production reprinted in Puttenham's *Art of English Poetry* about 1585.

are supposed to have happened in the play world itself. I have seen a modern parallel in pantomime. The "dame," addressing herself especially to the children, told them about the Demon King and his plans to steal her magic flower; if any attempt were to be made upon the flower, they must all cry out and bring her to the rescue. Uncontaminated by naturalistic theory (which, however, would be absorbed before School Certificate), and so unaware of any anomaly, they did cry out most heartily, and were obviously pleased to take an active part in the play. Such a ladder across from play world to real world can be explained only as an example of dual consciousness. If the person on the stage is simultaneously thought of as actor and as character, then it is possible to imagine him as actor, telling us about the story in which, as character, he is to take part. This is only a crude approach to the actual state of mind, which nowadays is best exemplified in the make-believe of children. If Tommy in a paper crown should claim to be king of the castle, his claim will be respected strictly for the purpose of play, but his identity will not be forgotten in the part, either by himself or his playfellows. I do not imply that the Elizabethans were childish or generally unsophisticated, only that their minds had not been warped by the naïve incredulity of scientific naturalism.

Soliloquy and Aside

Owing no doubt to Renaissance influence, direct address, in Shakespeare and the later Elizabethans, is normally softened to the familiar soliloquy and aside. These are usually explained as a conventional "thinking aloud,"[5] and might be regarded as a stage nearer than direct address to the goal of naturalism. Nonetheless, such

[5] The true nature of this "thinking" is discussed in Chapter IV, pp. 84-86.

speeches—and they include some of Shakespeare's greatest writing: the soliloquies of Hamlet, Iago, and Macbeth
—remain convincing only so long as the play world is
distinguished from the real world and allowed its own
code of behavior. Nor is it possible to draw a rigid line
between this conventional "thinking aloud" and the older
direct address. Listening to Hamlet as he debates the
time and manner of his uncle's death and discloses the
inconsistencies of his own nature, we may remember that
once, at a first performance, the famous Burbage, perhaps grown a trifle fattish and shortwinded, introduced
in this way his newest and most complex role to a repertory audience of largely familiar faces. To them, at
least, the soliloquies must have retained much of the
atmosphere of direct address. Indeed, if we examine
them, most soliloquies seem even verbally to carry this
suggestion of direct address, and it is a delicate matter
to distinguish their respective tones. "To be or not to be"
(*Hamlet*, III. i. 56) is reflective and best taken as "thinking aloud," though even here, as we have seen, there
must originally have been some feeling of immediate
communication with the audience. Iago certainly seems
to tell the audience directly of Othello's "free and open
nature" (I. iii. 389). The speech begins: "Thus do I
ever make my fool my purse," which sounds like explanation, not reflection; but it ends in "thinking aloud,"
though still, perhaps, with some suggestion of an audience:

> I have't. It is engender'd. Hell and night
> Must bring this monstrous birth to the world's light.
>
> (I. iii. 409)

The actor's mode of delivery will depend upon which
convention predominates: remote and detached for

"thinking aloud," intimate and confidential for direct address. Probably a combination of the two would in most
instances be truest to the original situation.

There are two types of aside to be distinguished. Of
the first are those remarks addressed by certain characters
to others and conventionally understood to be inaudible
to some further character or characters present on the
stage. Such, for instance, are the exclamations of the witnesses concealed in the box tree, when Malvolio discovers
and is deceived by Maria's letter. Fabian repeatedly calls
for silence, as Sir Toby and Sir Andrew explode in ridiculous threats; yet even Fabian, to be audible among the
audience, must be very distinctly audible to Malvolio
upon the stage. Malvolio's ignorance of their presence
is purely conventional, though admittedly such a convention was more manageable on a long Elizabethan
stage, with the audience packing close about it, than on
a picture-frame stage, where every "O, peace, peace!"
(*Twelfth Night*, II. v. 57) must be bellowed over the
orchestra pit.

The other type of aside is meant for the audience
only and is conventionally accepted as inaudible to other
characters upon the stage. Hamlet's "A little more than
kin, and less than kind" (I. ii. 65) corresponds to soliloquy of the "thinking aloud" class. A great many of these
asides come nearer to direct address. On the beach, as
Desdemona awaits Othello's arrival, she allows herself
to be amused by the cynical wit of Iago, who, playing
the bluff soldier, is "nothing, if not critical" (II. i. 120).
The audience, however, must not think her wanting in
the affectionate anxiety proper to her situation; it is important that they should never doubt for a moment her
fidelity and love. She must remain a pure-souled victim
of Iago's guile and Othello's stupidity. We are therefore

specially assured of her solicitude for Othello, as his ship struggles to harbor through the storm:

> I am not merry; but I do beguile
> The thing I am, by seeming otherwise,[6]
>
> (II. i. 123)

says Desdemona aside, before turning to Iago with apparent lightness: "Come, how wouldst thou praise me?" (II. i. 125.) This is not conventional thinking aloud. Shakespeare here is not making conscious feeling appear self-conscious; he is making unconscious feeling explicit. Desdemona does not think at all; her mind is employed with Iago's foolery so as to avoid thought. Her aside must be taken, then, as a direct word from playwright to audience, explaining mental processes of which Desdemona would herself, in reality, be only dimly aware.

Edgar saves the blinded Gloucester from suicide and despair by pretending to have led him to Dover Cliff, and later to have found him unharmed at its foot, when actually the old man has only thrown himself forward on to the level ground. There is a certain grim humor in the scene, and it is necessary that Edgar's benevolent purpose should be made plain: there must be no suggestion of a practical joke. He therefore explains himself to us in an aside which has the nature of direct statement:

> Why I do trifle thus with his despair
> Is done to cure it.[7]
>
> (*King Lear*, IV. vi. 33)

Since this type of aside occurs in *Othello* and in *Lear* itself, there is no valid reason—harking back to the

---

[6] Mentioned by Schücking, *op. cit.*, p. 224, and Bradbrook, *Elizabethan Stage Conditions*, p. 88.

[7] Mentioned by Schücking, *op. cit.*, p. 224.

first part of this chapter—to impugn the authenticity of the Fool's prophecy on account of its "primitive" technique. It is interesting to find these so-called "primitive" conventions in the tragic period: they can be no longer excused as 'prentice work, nor may they yet be ascribed to the weariness and disillusion which certain critics discover in the late romances. Shakespeare seems, in fact, always to have availed himself of such survivals of traditional technique; so that his increased use of them towards the end of his career merely witnesses to a belief in their vitality. In the last plays, they naturally accompany a return to the more conventional treatment of character and help to constitute a technical *simplesse* which is exploited for special purposes. Once naturalism usurped the serious stage, however, soliloquy and aside became a little absurd owing to the change in theater construction: a Victorian villain's shouted asides, hurled across the footlights and orchestra pit, must have borne little resemblance to Burbage's rapidly delivered confidences at the old Globe, with spectators crowding the apron all around him. From Victorian melodrama, the soliloquy and aside have passed into music hall and pantomime, where even architectural difficulties become negligible with an audience of limitless good will.

"Depersonalization"[8] *and Characters of Double Nature*

According to Professor Schücking[9] and others, the Elizabethan playwright was accustomed to indulge in "episodic intensification"—to concentrate on the scene in hand and its immediate effect, without too much regard for the total unity and consistency of his play. An Eliza-

---

[8] I take the term from Bradbrook, *Themes and Conventions of Elizabethan Tragedy*, p. 67.   [9] *Op. cit.*, chap. iv, pp. 111 f.

bethan play is often something of a variety performance, and the temptation to heighten immediate effects may not always have been resisted. This would account for what appear to be psychological inconsistencies in certain characters. Episodic intensification is particularly to be expected in those plays which were divided out, as often happened in the Elizabethan playhouse, among a number of hack writers, who worked on their own allotted portions, with only a very general notion of the plot as a whole. For reasons impossible to detail here, I believe that few, if any, of the plays recognized in the first folio as Shakespeare's were composed by this co-operative method. Nevertheless Shakespeare does provide examples of episodic intensification, especially in his earlier work, where, his purposes being less serious and his technique not yet secure, there is less subordination of parts to the whole. Even *Hamlet,* despite notorious complications in the Prince himself, is much more a variety show than the later tragedies: we have not only an avenger, but a ghost, a traveling theater, a mad scene, and a duel. There is a general lack of unity: the mad scene, for example, focuses more attention on Ophelia than her comparative unimportance in the plot would warrant; it may have been included principally because mad scenes were popular at the time. *Hamlet* betrays frequent signs of immaturity and experiment. To dispute the strength and depth and brilliance of the play would be absurd; but as poetic drama it cannot compare in quality with the later tragedies. Its greater popularity on the stage is due to sheer "entertainment value"; and it is a favorite with the critics because its imperfections leave more room for discussion, and the peculiar character of its hero provides a fascinating subject for every variety of armchair quackery.

Approached from what I believe to be the practical standpoint of audience psychology, *Hamlet* provides two excellent examples of the conventions I am to consider in this section. Depersonalization results from the simplest form of episodic intensification, where the writer has so concentrated on the content of a speech, as apparently to have ignored the speaker's identity. The Queen's description of Ophelia's death (*Hamlet*, IV. vii. 167) may best be understood in this way. Taking it naturalistically, we should have to speak of her as "softening" or "showing an unusual depth of sympathy"; to be thorough we should, of course, include her "poetic nature." On the same lines, a more sinister interpretation is possible, a *reductio ad absurdum* of the naturalistic approach. Why was Ophelia allowed to drown, if Gertrude, or whoever first reported the incident, was at hand to observe it so closely?[9a] We might well claim Gertrude as accessory after the fact; and her speech then becomes both hypocritical and an ingenuous, if tacit, admission of her own negligence and guilt. Even approaching the matter with due regard for Shakespeare's conventional treatment of character, we are bound to concede a certain inconsistency. Gertrude's account of Ophelia is presumably similar in principle to the villain's recognition of the hero's virtues; it is an objective statement, with no psychological implication. Nevertheless, it differs from Oliver on Orlando, for example, since, in its whole length, there is no reference to the speaker's own nature, but attention is entirely concentrated on Ophelia, whose death is described with lyrical emotion. Gertrude loses her identity during an entire speech, so that she may perform the part of messenger to inform us of Ophelia's end. Such depersonalization is purely a matter of convenience and economy. It is rendered plausible by the poetry; there is nothing

[9a] Cf. Bradbrook, *op. cit.*, p. 90.

in its elegiac strains to remind us of the queen who exchanged "Hyperion for a satyr" (I. ii. 140).

The satyr himself, King Claudius, has one scene in which, through episodic intensification, he is endowed with a character quite different from that which normally he sustains. Claudius is the villain of the piece, a smiling villain, with a suave, disarming manner; but faced with the Laertes uprising, he suddenly displays a surprising combination of quiet courage and royal dignity:

> What is the cause, Laertes,
> That thy rebellion looks so giant-like?
> Let him go, Gertrude; do not fear our person:
> There's such divinity doth hedge a king,
> That treason can but peep to what it would,
> Acts little of his will. Tell me, Laertes,
> Why thou art thus incensed. Let him go, Gertrude.
> Speak, man.
>
> (IV. v. 120)

This apparent change of nature may, of course, be explained on sound psychological principles; but such an explanation would scarcely be consistent with the usual simplicity of Shakespeare's characterization. The alternative is episodic intensification, this time sustained throughout an episode of some length.[10] Hamlet, the real hero, is off the stage—gone a prisoner to England; we already have a villain in Laertes, or at least an exhibition of lawless and uncontrolled fury; and a scene is always better for the strong contrast of two opponents. Claudius falls naturally into the hero's role. Moreover, in those days a good royalist could hardly refuse so admirable an opportunity to present royalty at its best, standing calm and superior, hedged with divinity against the forces of rebellion and disorder. The old Claudius is therefore set

[10] There is a suggestion of this view in Schücking, *op. cit.*, p. 175.

aside for a time, replaced by a dignified figure with whom we are bound to sympathize; the scene itself is strengthened, and any political feeling aroused is strictly as it ought to be.

King Claudius is metamorphosed for part of a scene, his double nature being due to episodic intensification at one point; but in *As You Like It,* Touchstone has two irreconcilable "characters," which are held in parallel throughout the play. The question of episodic intensification does not arise, since both "characters" may function in the same scene, or indeed at the same time. On his first entry and before he speaks, Celia refers to Touchstone as "this natural" and observes that "always the dullness of the fool is the whetstone of the wits" (I. ii. 57). When he does speak, however, we are surprised to find him, not a natural, but a mordantly satirical wit. His first jest is of the knight, who swore by his honor and was not forsworn, "for he never had any" (I. ii. 83); and shortly afterwards his good sense is displayed in the timely rebuke which answers Monsieur Le Beau's invitation to the ladies to watch a wrestling match: "Thus men grow wiser every day: it is the first time that ever I heard breaking of ribs was sport for ladies" (I. ii. 145). As the Duke says later: "He uses his folly like a stalking-horse and under the presentation of that he shoots his wit" (V. iv. 111). If, then, we take Celia's characterization of him objectively and believe it, Touchstone must be accepted as both fool and wit—like Falstaff "not only witty in himself, but the cause that wit is in other men" (*II Henry IV,* I. ii. 11).

This definition once accepted, the behavior of Touchstone becomes intelligible. *As You Like It* is an artificial play, a play in which the complex love tangle can be solved, and daughter greet long-lost father, all in the rhyming course of a Masque of Hymen. It is in fact no more naturalistic than *The Mikado*. On the highest moral grounds we might condemn Yum-yum for breaking her engagement at the prospect of being buried alive; or alternatively we might condemn Gilbert for inconsistency in his outline of a girl of high spirit and resolve ("I mean to rule the earth, As he the sky"). There is, however, rather more music in *The Mikado* than in *As You Like It*, perhaps enough to have lulled the moral and psychological susceptibilities of the critics. For there are those who regard Touchstone as a psychological problem, and to whom the Audrey marriage is fraught with profound significance. Why should a wit and a wise man, one endowed with such insight as to be the touchstone by whom the rest are tried, seek to ally himself with this rustic ignoramus, who had already found her true match in the dull-witted William? It is Touchstone's final cynicism, they say, to "press in...amongst the rest of the country copulatives" (V. iv. 57) and claim this "poor virgin," this "ill-favoured thing," as his own. It is an acted comment on the romantical attachments of the others: stripped of the high-falutin', where is the difference between this union of Touchstone and Audrey and the other three marriages for which a Masque of Hymen had been designed?

> Birth, and copulation, and death,
>   I'd be bored.
>   You'd be bored.
> Birth, and copulation, and death.[11]

Did Shakespeare, in Touchstone, anticipate Mr. Eliot's reading of the twentieth-century materialistic mind?

[11] T. S. Eliot, "Fragment of an Agon," *Collected Poems 1909-1935* (London: Faber & Faber, 1936).

To meet such critics on their own ground, we can at least say that, if Touchstone married Audrey as a symbolic warning to the rest and saddled himself with an undesirable wife in order to underline his cynical philosophy, then he is certainly not the wise man we have taken him for. Again, Touchstone's easy jests upon courtship and marriage were hardly intended to go very deep; his attitude is characteristic of all professional entertainers, who know that serious things always provide the best jokes: courtship and marriage are their most popular subjects, but they are closely followed by the themes of birth and death and what comes after death. Their flippancy is successful just because of its incongruity with our deepest feelings. There is nothing new in Touchstone's verdict upon love, and nothing sinister in his tone, that we should take him more seriously than his fellow entertainers: "We that are true lovers run into strange capers; but as all is mortal in nature, so is all nature in love mortal in folly" (II. iv. 54). He is no pathological cynic, such as would spite his own base desires with an ill-assorted marriage.[12]   One wonders whether such creatures existed before the vogue of psychoanalysis; they certainly have not an Elizabethan ring. A notion of this kind would never occur to Shakespeare; but if it had occurred to him, and he had decided to make use of it, he would have stated the position very clearly, without ambiguity or indirections. He would never have left an Elizabethan audience to worry out so unusual a conception by inductive methods in the naturalistic way.

The true explanation of Touchstone's behavior lies in the psychology, not of Touchstone himself, but of the audience. Professional jesters are witty, but they are also fools: they are to be laughed *at* as well as *with;* and

[12] James Smith, "As You Like It," *Scrutiny*, IX (June, 1940), 9-32.

if they "wear not motley in their brains" (*Twelfth Night*, I. v. 63), it is up to them not to let their public behavior be unduly influenced by their natural good sense. The audience would expect to laugh at Touchstone, the court jester—not to sympathize with him. Shakespeare makes him witty because we do not tire of wit as we do of the "natural." William and Audrey provide the dullness—but again, a highly stylized dullness, funnier than nature—and they have very little of the dialogue. Touchstone, in a fat part, must have wit; but there is no reason why he should not be a fool also, in the matter of Audrey, and so constitute a double source of amusement. The psychological difficulty is brushed aside, and we are given a character wise in speech and foolish in action—which seems to have been the character usually assumed by a court jester. The audience is thus required to attend simultaneously to two diverse aspects of a situation, and to keep the two strands of attention separate; to enjoy the folly and the wit without any naturalistic sense of their incompatibility.

The conventions of depersonalization and of "double nature" (both the Claudius and the Touchstone varieties) obviously depend upon a dual consciousness of play world and real world; but even in a conventional theater, they are not entirely satisfactory. Ideally, plot, character, and dialogue should be closely interrelated, and the themes of a play be expressed through their fusion at every point. When a single character is made to do double service, the associations gathered around his first personality have to be thrust aside for his second personality to function; uncertainty and a degree of disharmony are bound to result. Significantly, it is in the earlier plays that these conventions occur most frequently, and in plays which are not organized into a complete poetic and dramatic unity. I have mentioned the uncertain structure of *Hamlet;* and in *As You Like It* there is some discontinuity between the levels of plot, character, and dialogue. Its deeper themes are conveyed mainly in the dialogue, and almost incidentally: the concern with court *versus* country and the question of literary pastoral. There is a triple burlesque: of the courtiers who sigh for the country (the Duke at the end leaves his "sermons in stones" (II. i. 17) with an indecent haste); of the pastoral convention in literature (in the dialogue of Silvius and Phebe); and of the country itself (in the clodhopping rudeness of William and Audrey). It is the serious tone distinguishing at times his treatment of Corin and Adam that leads us to see where Shakespeare's true sympathies lie—with the old rural order, which in his own lifetime was being rapidly displaced by commercial enterprise. A profound comment upon this process comes very casually in a remark of Corin:

> . . . I am shepherd to another man
> And do not shear the fleeces that I graze:
> My master is of churlish disposition
> And little recks to find the way to heaven
> By doing deeds of hospitality.
>
> (II. iv. 78)

Rosalind in Arden may perhaps represent the true blend of court and country, but there is no inevitable relationship between the romantic plot and what I take to be the underlying theme. Shakespeare's chief purpose was entertainment, his deeper purpose only incidental, and so it would be wrong to take everything in the play as equally significant. In such circumstances, there is no harm in Touchstone's double nature; we are not to treat matters of character very seriously. Sometimes Touchstone's dialogue is relevant to the deeper theme, and we must not reject this incidental wisdom because of his foolish behavior on other occasions.

In the later plays, depersonalization may occur occasionally in a minor character, e.g., the episode in which Enobarbus describes Cleopatra to his Roman acquaintances; but I do not know of any "double natures" on a major scale. Professor Schücking considers Cleopatra herself to have two distinct "characters" through episodic intensification; there is discontinuity, he thinks, between the wanton of the earlier scenes and the tragic queen who triumphs in adversity. I hope, however, to show in the next chapter that this judgment results from his over-naturalistic approach to a character expressed almost wholly by poetic means. Professor Stoll's interpretation of the tragic heroes is a variant upon the double nature hypothesis. But in the mature tragedies, Shakespeare's integration is very close; the themes are exactly worked out on the levels of plot, character, and dialogue, which are all fused into a poetic and dramatic whole. Again, whereas the comic themes are relatively intellectual and capable of detached treatment as ideas within the dialogue, the tragedies are concerned with man's metaphysical destiny, and one or two principal characters serve as an universal symbol of human nature. Through them, as they are presented in poetry, the theme is developed. It is therefore essential that they should be self-consistent, since in this and all other respects they must correspond to the general experience of mankind. Shakespeare cannot be understood without due attention to the conventions he employs, but just as there was danger in pushing psychological analysis too far, there is a danger also of being hagridden by conventions.

Allegory and Symbol in Character Presentation

The Elizabethan drama's sudden efflorescence and its rapidly attained maturity have tended to distract attention from the dramatic tradition out of which it developed, and to which it must have been bound by the strongest ligaments of organic growth.   Miracle plays were still performed in Shakespeare's youth, and moralities continued to be produced well into the second half of the sixteenth century. It is very important to realize that the degree of representationalism attained in Shakespeare's characters was something quite new, and that an elderly member of the Globe audience might be more familiar with personified virtues and vices than with the newfangled character types. Moreover, transition from allegorical figures to the ordinary stage types was a gradual process, like the transition from types to individuals in the nineteenth century. Falstaff at the Boar's Head undertakes a burlesque "in King Cambyses' vein" (*I Henry IV*, II. iv. 425): by the time of Shakespeare's *Henry IV*, "King Cambyses" might have well become a figure of fun; but at least he was still remembered by the average theatergoer, or Falstaff's burlesque would have fallen flat. *Cambises* was written by one Thomas Preston, somewhere between 1560 and 1569.[13]   It is a crude tragedy of blood in the popular romantic manner, written in the old "fourteeners," and without any intrinsic merit; but it is remarkable in having personifications of the morality type mingled with its ordinary characters. The scene is set at the Persian court, where we have such characters as King Cambises himself; Smirdis, his brother; Sisamnes, the judge, and so on. Humor is, however, provided by a Vice, Ambidexter, who, like

---

[13] Adams (ed.), *op. cit.*, p. 638, n. 1.

Groucho Marx, informs the audience that he has forgotten his name:

> Ha! my name? My name would ye so faine know?
> Yea, iwis, shal ye, and that with al speed!—
> I have forgot it, therefore I cannot show.
> A! a! now I have it! I have it, in-deed!
> My name is Ambidexter. I signifie one
> That with both hands finely can play.[14]

Although his name has allegorical significance, Ambidexter is almost a representational character. Other figures are more completely allegorical: Shame describes the King's misdeeds; the people complain against an unjust judge, not through a deputation of angry citizens, but by means of two allegorical characters, Commons Cry and Commons Complaint; Proof and Triall convict the judge, and Execution finishes their work. The king's brother is attended by Attendance and Diligence: and Cruelty and Murder are employed as assassins. An audience at the first performance of *King Henry IV, Part I*, would remember when a curious medley of allegory and representation, such as *Cambises*, was quite acceptable to them, and though with changing fashion they would be prepared to laugh at the Falstaff burlesque, it is unlikely that their fundamental habits of attention had entirely changed.

Specifically in relation to character, I use the term "allegory" to signify the representation of a virtue or vice or of some other abstraction, by a stage personage. I regard a character as symbolic when it successfully and permanently embodies some great truth of human experience, or when it expresses some aspect or aspects of

[14] Ll. 146 ff., in *ibid.*, p. 644.

the Deity in His relations with mankind.[15] Shakespeare nowhere introduces characters which are overtly allegorical, but his representational characters frequently have about them a suggestion of allegory or symbol. As Ambidexter, the Vice, is almost a representational character, so in Shakespeare certain representational characters may be said at times to become almost allegorical—there has been more change in intention than in actual performance. The Vice is generally recognized as an ancestor of the Shakespearean clown, but the character in Shakespeare most resembling the Vice is undoubtedly Thersites.

Troilus and Cressida is a consciously philosophical play. Normally Shakespeare's philosophical notions are incarnated in character and action; and his poetic thought, always concrete and image-filled, relates to character and action directly, and only indirectly to whatever general truths may be implied. The "To-morrow and to-morrow" speech (V. v. 19) expresses directly Macbeth's reaction to his wife's death and merely implies the atheism ("dusty death," "Signifying nothing") which has resulted from his gradual hardening in crime. In *Troilus and Cressida*, on the other hand, the thought, only partially embodied in character and action, flows over into the dialogue, which, though usually concrete enough and full of imagery, is frequently developed almost independently of the situation to which it refers. Ulysses' great speech on "degree" (*Troilus and Cressida*, I. iii. 75) begins and ends with Troy, but is much more concerned with generalities of political philosophy than with the Trojan war; in *Troilus and Cressida* the story is an excuse for thought rather than the embodiment of thought. The

[15] Cf. the account of "The Great Commonplaces" and of Symbol, in E. M. W. Tillyard, *Poetry Direct and Oblique* (London: Chatto & Windus, 1934), Part I, chap. iii, pp. 22 f.; chap. iv, pp. 54 f.; and Part III, chap. iii, pp. 167 f.

metaphysical problems of the tragedies must, from the first, have presented themselves to Shakespeare in terms of concrete experience; but in *Troilus and Cressida* he pursues philosophical abstractions with the impassioned eagerness of Donne. Problems of time and value and their mutual relations are thrust forward for the audience's attention:

> Time hath, my lord, a wallet at his back,
> Wherein he puts alms for oblivion.
>
> (III. iii. 145)

As in Donne, philosophy is usually apprehended in terms of sense experience, but occasionally even the bare bones of abstract thinking appear, for example, in Troilus' crucial but awkward query: "What is aught, but as 'tis valued?" (II. ii. 52.)

In such a play it is no wonder to find characters with something of a "morality" flavor. As Thersites recalls the old Vice, so Ulysses conveys some suggestion of an abstract Worldly Wisdom. Most of the characters in *Troilus and Cressida* express themselves philosophically, but Ulysses has an especially large share of such speeches, including the famous "degree" speech and the speech on Time. With him even more than the others, what he says is infinitely more important than why he says it, and at times even his behavior is hard to interpret on naturalistic grounds. When Cressida arrives in the Grecian camp, Agamemnon receives her with a kiss: "Our general doth salute you with a kiss," says Nestor (IV. v. 19). Ulysses comments with a pun:

> Yet is the kindness but particular;
> 'Twere better she were kiss'd in general.
>
> (IV. v. 20)

The others act upon this advice, and Cressida is kissed in turn by all the Greek leaders. When his own turn comes, however, there is a short wit battle in which Ulysses insultingly rejects the kiss that Cressida is presumably willing to give:

> *Ulyss.*: May I, sweet lady, beg a kiss of you?
> *Cres.*: You may.
> *Ulyss.*:   I do desire it.
> *Cres.*:   Why, beg, then.
> *Ulyss.*: Why then for Venus' sake, give me a kiss,
>   When Helen is a maid again, and his [*sc.* Menelaus'].
> *Cres.*: I am your debtor, claim it when 'tis due.
> *Ulyss.*: Never's my day, and then a kiss of you.
>   (IV. v. 47)

When Diomedes leads Cressida away, Ulysses bursts into denunciation:

>   Fie, fie upon her!
> There's language in her eye, her cheek, her lip,
> Nay, her foot speaks; her wanton spirits look out
> At every joint and motive of her body.
> O, these encounterers, so glib of tongue,
> That give accosting welcome ere it comes,
> And wide unclasp the tables of their thoughts
> To every ticklish reader! set them down
> For sluttish spoils of opportunity
> And daughters of the game.
>   (IV. v. 54)

Speaking naturalistically, we should admire this moral rectitude more heartily, if Ulysses had not himself initiated the general kissing. Taken conventionally, however, the incident is central to the Troilus-Cressida theme. The handing over of Cressida to the Greeks is the handing over of Troilus' ideal love to the sullying of the world; we are to be prepared for his betrayal, and our knowledge of Cressida's character must be so established that no psychological doubt remain to befog the philosophical issue. Ulysses, at least during this incident (episodic intensification again!), represents an impersonal Wisdom, whose judgment we must accept. He devises a test for Cressida which sufficiently reveals her character and the character of those she has come among; and his own refusal to kiss her sets him apart from the others, in judicial aloofness, so that we are prepared to accept the verdict which he pronounces after Cressida is led away. The whole passage is in rhyme and full of wordplay: this not only emphasizes the tone of badinage and flirtation, but also serves to distance or frame the whole incident, which thus appears in a sort of vocal italics to draw attention to its symbolic function. To condemn Ulysses' conduct as ungentlemanly would be to attribute to the character a representational quality which the passage seems to disallow. There is a suggestion of deity about Ulysses; we must accept his moral judgments, but we must not search the morality of his own conduct, which is, as it were, an Olympian setting of the stage for human conflict. As the embodiment of wisdom, he is to be praised or blamed solely in reference to that one quality. It is only at times that this hint of allegory appears in the action and dialogue of Ulysses: Shakespeare's reversion to an older technique is probably unconscious; but it is nonetheless interesting on that account.

Troilus and Cressida, as probably the most intellectual of Shakespeare's plays, reveals an unusually high degree of conventionalism in the presentation of character; examples can be found of most of the conventions discussed in this chapter and the last. Thersites, whose relation to the Vice has already been mentioned, might perhaps best be classed as a "humor," his predominant characteristic being a cynical and prurient wit. Lechery is his favorite

theme: "Nothing but lechery! all incontinent varlets!"
(V. i. 105.) He does duty also as a scurrilous chorus upon the futility of war—a role comparable to that of Falstaff in the battle scenes of *Henry IV, Part I*. His remark
above occurs significantly at the end of a scene, and the
next scene closes with a similar but even more emphatic
outburst: "Lechery, lechery; still, wars and lechery;
nothing else holds fashion: a burning devil take them!"
(V. ii. 195.) To close two successive scenes of the fifth
act in this way is surely to commend the opinion of Thersites to our very serious attention. Ajax and Achilles are
practically humours: senseless vanity and strength in
Ajax; selfish pride and strength in Achilles. Helen is
also a humour: in the one scene in which she appears,
her only characteristic is a weak and silly sex-obsession:
"Let thy song be love: this love will undo us all. O
Cupid, Cupid, Cupid!" (II. i. 119.) Professor Wilson
Knight is surely mistaken in considering her to be a
worthy object of Trojan idealism.[16] This scene, which is
almost central in position, is certainly central at any rate
to one theme of the play: the theme of "fair without and
foul within," which I shall later treat more fully. The
Helen whose face had launched a thousand Marlovian
ships is subjected to a remorseless Shakespearean "de-
bunking"; in a few lines the real Helen is revealed, the
inadequate object of so much misplaced idealism. Other
characters in the play are more complex, though none is
seen very clearly in the round.

An interesting example of depersonalization occurs
in Diomedes, the careless and sensual Greek, to whom
Cressida so quickly transfers herself. It is he who rises

---

[16] So at least he implies, in speaking of this scene: ". . . the strains of
music," he says, "herald the entry of Helen, queen of romance" (*The
Wheel of Fire*, p. 67).

above the spite and misrepresentation of war, in pity for both sides, and condemns, with remarkable moral fervor, the unworthy cause of the whole dispute:

> For every false drop in her bawdy veins
> A Grecian's life hath sunk; for every scruple
> Of her contaminated carrion weight,
> A Trojan hath been slain: since she could speak,
> She has not given so many good words breath
> As for her Greeks and Trojans suffer'd death.
>
> (IV. i. 69)

This is an unusually clearsighted view of the matter, but it is also extremely discourteous, as it is addressed to the culprit, Paris, and Diomedes has come under a flag of truce. But Paris takes it very quietly, and replies:

> Fair Diomed, you do as chapmen do,
> Dispraise the thing that you desire to buy.
>
> (IV. i. 75)

The reference to chapmen—hawkers of cheap goods—confirms, despite the speaker, the attitude to Helen which Diomedes has already expressed. Clearly Diomedes here steps out of character, and Paris also speaks truer than he knows.

Action as well as character may be symbolic, even action which is not represented on the stage. Paris' request that Helen should "help unarm our Hector" (III. i. 163) clinches the Helen scene and assures its central position. The outward show of chivalry is there; but we know Hector to be the worthiest of the Trojans, and Helen a worthless strumpet. That Hector should yield to fight in such a cause is the undoing of himself and of Troy: that Helen should play the role of his "fair lady" —a Helen who can be so much at home with Pandarus— is the height of Shakespearean irony. In the play's last

act, action and character mingle in what is unique in
Shakespeare—a direct allegorical presentation of his dramatic theme. Hector, despite the entreaties of Andromache, and the prophetic warnings of Cassandra, joins
the battle, as his honor bids him. The usual battle confusion is presented in what modern editors unnecessarily
divide into a series of short scenes. Near the end of scene
vi there is a stage direction which reads, in our modern
editions, *"Enter one in sumptuous armour."* In the
Quarto and Folios, it is simply *"Enter one in armour,"*[17]
but Malone's addition of "sumptuous"[18] merely underlines Shakespeare's obvious intention, for Hector cries
out to this anonymous figure:

> Stand, stand, thou Greek; thou art a goodly mark:
> No? Wilt thou not? I like thy armour well;
> I'll frush it and unlock the rivets all,
> But I'll be master of it: wilt thou not, beast, abide?
> Why, then fly on, I'll hunt thee for thy hide.
>
> (V. vi. 27)

At the beginning of scene viii, we find Hector presumably standing over the mysterious person whom he has
now slain, and saying:

> Most putrefied core, so fair without,
> Thy goodly armour thus hath cost thy life.
> Now is my day's work done; I'll take good breath:
> Rest, sword; thou hast thy fill of blood and death.
>
> (V. viii. 1)

At this point *"Enter Achilles and Myrmidons,"* and Hector meets his death unarmed at the hands of the cowardly
hero and his pack. We hear from Troilus, two scenes
later, that

[17] See *Troilus and Cressida*, in *The Cambridge Shakespeare*, ed. William Aldis Wright (London: Macmillan & Co., Ltd., 1894), p. 159, note
to l. 27.   [18] See n. 19.

He's dead; and at the murderer's horse's tail,
In beastly sort, dragg'd through the shameful field.

(V. x. 4)

Shakespeare took the incident of the "one in sumptuous
armour" from Lydgate's *Troye Boke*,[19] but seems to have
given it a wider significance. The crucial question here
is, "Why 'putrefied core'?"[20] There is nothing in
Lydgate to explain this remarkable apostrophe. What
did Shakespeare intend by it? The "one in sumptuous
armour" was surely not dead when he first entered, and
he had had no time to putrefy after being killed. Or
does it mean that he was old, or diseased, or infirm?
In any event, Hector had won the armor which he
coveted, so why this apparently embittered comment?
I do not see any naturalistic explanation. What I suggest is that Shakespeare saw in the incident in Lydgate
an allegory similar to the "whited sepulchre" of Holy
Scripture: "sumptuous armour" stands for the "outward show" which covers an inner corruption. Perhaps
with the scriptural passage in mind, Shakespeare ren-

[19] See Steevens's note, in Malone's edition of Shakespeare (1821),
VIII, 437:
"This circumstance is taken from Lydgate's poem, p. 196:
'—Guido in his historic doth shew
By worthy Hector's fall, who coveting
To have the sumptuous armour of the king, etc.
So greedy was thereof, that when he had
The body up, and on his horse it bare,
To have the spoil thereof such haste he made
That he did hang his shield without all care
Behind him at his back, the easier
To pull the armour off at his desire,
And by that means his breast clean open lay,' etc.
"This furnished Shakespeare with the hint for the following line:
'I am unarm'd; forego this vantage, Greek.'"
Malone obviously borrowed the epithet "sumptuous" from Steevens's
quotation or its original.
[20] The word is "core," not "corse," and implies a metaphor from
rotten fruit.

dered his symbol complete by adding the "putrefied core," although the reference is incapable of natural explanation, and must be taken by the audience on an entirely different plane from the rest of the play. The "sumptuous armour" with its "putrefied core" thus becomes a symbol of all the play presents to us, an allegorical enactment of the theme of "fair without, and foul within," which is applicable almost everywhere in the Troy and Troilus stories as Shakespeare rewrites them. It applies to the war, with its false chivalry and inadequate aim; to Helen, to Cressida, and a good many more of the personages involved; and it applies, lastly, to the death of Hector, with which it is so closely linked in presentation. Hector was the best of the Trojans, and better than the best of the Greeks: he saw, most clearly of them all, the essential evil of the war, waged to keep Helen from her lawful husband:

> . . . 'tis mad idolatry
> To make the service greater than the god,
>
> (II. ii. 56)

he said. And yet he concluded for the continuation of the war:

> For 'tis a cause that hath no mean dependance
> Upon our joint and several dignities.
>
> (II. ii. 192)

Later, he ignored Andromache and Cassandra, in order to fulfil the supposed duties of a false conception of honor. Unworthy aims are bound to tarnish the most chivalrous nature: and so Hector himself, a few moments before he is brutally murdered, so far loses his chivalric courtesy as to call out "beast" after the "one in sumptuous armour," and then: "I'll hunt thee for thy hide"— the least worthy of motives. His death and the shameful treatment of his corpse are perhaps punishment in excess of his swerving, but they point sharply to the previous degradation he had suffered. Even in the *Troye Boke,* there is at least a suggestion that Hector's death was in some sense a consequence of his greed. Shakespeare elaborates the incident, places it at the climax of his play, and removes all possibility of natural explanation, so that he surely meant it to bear the extended significance which I have suggested. Otherwise there seems no point in his choice of this particular incident when so many important happenings in the Troy story are necessarily omitted, and absolutely no point in the further complication of the "putrefied core."

Troilus and Cressida is thus a play which especially calls for the exercise of multiconsciousness. In addition to the usual dual consciousness of play world and real world, and of past and present time, there is the dual consciousness of story and philosophy, since the two are not wholly merged; there is the dual consciousness of character as representative and as allegorical; and further, there must be a dual consciousness of certain incidents in their naturalistic and their allegorical significances.

It is unnecessary to deal at length with the symbolic aspects of character; they have been discussed a good deal by other writers, and I have said something upon the subject myself in the previous chapter. It has been generally recognized that a great character, such as Lear or Macbeth, is not merely the portrait of an individual, but has the significance of representative humanity. What has not been sufficiently realized is the selective method by which such symbolism is achieved: that, as I have already shown, Lear and Macbeth are not fully individualized, but in them certain common human characteristics are selectively presented: Lear's blind self-will, which is purged by suffering; Macbeth's "vaulting ambition" (I. vii. 27), which hardens into bloodthirsty tyranny. By concentrating dramatic attention upon them, and by a poetic heightening of their deeds and sufferings, they are posed for us centrally and in the limelight. The capital error is to ascribe their powerful effect to some special psychological insight. Shakespeare has a certain insight into psychological detail, but it is revealed only occasionally: his real insight is into the general nature of experience, and his power is a poetic and dramatic power by which the responses of an audience are directed and controlled.

Characters may also be symbolic of some aspects of Deity. There are, I believe, only two examples of this, and both have been commented upon by previous writers. Professor Wilson Knight, in his essay on *Measure for Measure* in *The Wheel of Fire*, gives excellent reasons for taking the Duke as to some degree representing God's providence. He goes about unrecognized among his people, guiding and controlling their destinies, and bringing good out of evil in the end. The play abounds in theological language; even the humor is theological: the second scene of Act I begins with "the sanctimonious pirate, that went to sea with the Ten Commandments" (I. ii. 7), and goes on to a punning discussion of grace before meat and "grace" in its theological sense. At the end of the play, in what Professor Knight sees as a temporal representation of the Last Judgment,[21] Angelo, when his wicked courses have been discovered, says to the Duke:

> . . . I perceive your grace, like power divine,
> Hath look'd upon my passes—
>
> (V. i. 374)

[21] *The Wheel of Fire*, p. 91.

which shows that, whether consciously or not, a comparison of the Duke to "power divine" had been running in Shakespeare's mind. (Also, in its context, "your grace" probably implies more than a formal mode of address.) Prospero is the other character who seems to represent divine providence. He again engineers the whole plot so that good may come out of evil, and he foreknows the happy outcome of his plans. When Miranda complains to him:

> O, I have suffered
> With those that I saw suffer. . .
> (*The Tempest*, I. ii. 5)

(in the ship which has apparently just been sunk), Prospero is able to reply:

> Be collected:
> No more amazement: tell your piteous heart
> There's no harm done.
> (I. ii. 13)

Prospero, indeed, is returning good for evil; more than that, out of his very suffering, joy and prosperity have been wrought for all. Old Gonzalo sums up the moral in a speech I have already had occasion to quote:

> Was Milan thrust from Milan, that his issue
> Should become kings of Naples? O, rejoice
> Beyond a common joy. . . .
> (V. i. 205)

The theological parallel is again too close to be accidental. Yet both the Duke in *Measure for Measure*, and Prospero, are endowed with characteristics which make it impossible for us to regard them as direct representations of the Deity, such as we find in the miracle plays. They are human beings, however they may signify the divine; and Prospero at least, has human imperfections: thus he

temporarily forgets Caliban's plot against him (IV. i.
139), and says later:

> Sir, I am vex'd;
> Bear with my weakness; my old brain is troubled:
> Be not disturb'd with my infirmity:
> If you be pleased, retire into my cell
> And there repose: a turn or two I'll walk,
> To still my beating mind.
>
> (IV. i. 158)

Again the audience needs to attend simultaneously to two
diverse aspects of the same character: the representational
and the symbolic.

CHAPTER VI

FURTHER RAMIFICATIONS OF MULTICONSCIOUSNESS

Comedy and Tragedy Mixed

THE MIXTURE of comedy and tragedy, so often debated by critics who take their *Poetics* seriously, is founded psychologically on the popular audience's ability to shift rapidly its modes of attention; and this ability is merely the exercise of multiconsciousness in temporal succession. Furthermore, such rapid shifts of viewpoint are possible only when consciousness of the play as play safeguards the audience from any expectation of naturalism. "Comic relief" has always characterized the popular dramatic tradition, from the time when religious drama, gaining relative freedom in the churchyard, began to develop the comic possibilities of Noah's wife and of the multitude of fiends necessary for the harrowing of hell. In the *Secunda Pastorum* of the Towneley cycle,[1] we have contrasting comic and serious scenes, like the Jacobean antimasque and masque. The shepherds first visit Mak's house in search of a sheep which they suspect him of having stolen. Mak, who has concealed the sheep in a cradle, pretends that it is a newly born baby. The visitors insist on paying their respects to this new arrival; there are suitable comments on the facial peculiarities of so unusual a child; and, the fraud being unmasked, Mak is tossed in a sheet. Then, after this hilarious scene, the shepherds return to the fields and, hearing the angels' song, hasten to Bethlehem where they worship the Holy Child, offering their simple gifts.

[1] Adams (ed.), *op. cit.*, pp. 145 f.

Shakespeare's comic relief is traditional but more subtle. We laugh at the gravediggers (*Hamlet*, V. i), before passing to the graveside meeting of Hamlet and Laertes; but we already suspect from the dialogue that it is Ophelia's grave they are preparing, and so are aware simultaneously of tragedy and comedy. This presence of dramatic irony renders the term "comic relief" inadequate here: double consciousness not only functions in quick transition, but is called on for a simultaneous appraisal of two aspects of the comic situation itself. Nor does comedy entirely disappear from the scene when tragic emotion enters, for there is a grotesque comedy in the exaggerated language of Laertes:

> Now pile your dust upon the quick and dead,
> Till of this flat a mountain you have made,
> To o'ertop old Pelion, or the skyish head
> Of blue Olympus—
>
> (V. i. 274)

a comedy which jars on the fine ear of Hamlet and makes him rave in hyperbolic rivalry:

> Woo't weep? woo't fight? woo't fast? woo't tear thyself?
> Woo't drink up eisel? eat a crocodile?
>
> (V. i. 298)

Again, in *Macbeth*, the Porter scene is more than "comic interlude"; its theme and atmosphere are appropriate to a play concerned so deeply with the supernatural and the eternal validity of human choice. The far-reaching significance of the "equivocator" reference has already been considered. The grotesque humor of *Lear*, as Professor Wilson Knight has shown,[2] permeates some of the play's most tragic scenes; for if we are to sympathize with struggling humanity, we are to see at the same time that

[2] See "Lear and the Comedy of the Grotesque," *The Wheel of Fire*, pp. 175 f.

much of the struggle is folly proceeding from lack of faith. Gloucester's attempted suicide has a certain crude comedy on the stage: the old man falls not over a cliff, as he imagines, but forward on to the level ground—on to the stage boards, in fact. Edgar assures him "Thy life's a miracle" (IV. vi. 55), and describes a comically fearsome fiend as having tried to lure him to his death, only to be foiled by "the clearest gods" (IV. vi. 73). Of such stuff Gloucester's conversion is effected:

> . . . henceforth [he says] I'll bear
> Affliction till it do cry out itself
> "Enough, enough," and die.
>
> (IV. vi. 75)

This is the profound humor of religious faith; our direst perils are like the stumble of a blind old man, who in his blindness sees a cliff face where "the clearest gods" have prepared smooth ground for an easy fall. So much, again, for the bitter agnosticism read by so many critics into the religious attitudes of *King Lear*.

There is one scene which is usually omitted from modern productions of *Romeo and Juliet:* the scene in which the Capulet household mourn Juliet's supposed death after she has taken Friar Laurence's potion. When Mr. Terence Gray had the play performed in the Festival Theater at Cambridge, without the usual cuts, this scene was treated as burlesque. Indignant letters showered on the producer, whose reply was to quote from the scene itself:

> O woe! O woful, woful, woful day!
> Most lamentable day, most woful day!
> That ever, ever, I did yet behold!
> O day! O day! O day! O hateful day!
> Never was seen so black a day as this:
> O woful day, O woful day!
>
> (IV. v. 49)

This is the Nurse, but Lady Capulet is little better with her "Accursed, unhappy, wretched, hateful day!" (IV. v. 43) and her frequent repetitions:

> But one, poor one, one poor and loving child
> But one thing to rejoice and solace in.
>
> (IV. v. 46)

Paris also has an imposing list of epithets and a passage of stilted and balanced repetition:

> Beguiled, divorced, wronged, spited, slain!
> Most detestable death, by thee beguiled,
> By cruel, cruel thee quite overthrown!
> O love! O life! not life, but love in death!
>
> (IV. v. 55)

And Capulet follows in the same manner, beginning with the list of epithets and going on to his rhetorically balanced repetitions:

> Despised, distressed, hated, martyr'd, kill'd!
> Uncomfortable time, why camest thou now
> To murder, murder our solemnity?
> O child! O child! my soul, and not my child!
> Dead art thou! Alack! my child is dead;
> And with my child my joys are buried.
>
> (IV. v. 59)

Romeo and Juliet is an early play and not one of Shakespeare's best; he uses too freely the conventionally conceited manner of Petrarchan love poetry. But comparison with Romeo's last big speech in the tomb, faulty though it is by the standard of Shakespeare's own later work, will show that these lamentations over the supposed corpse of Juliet cannot have been intended to move compassion in his audience. The tone of burlesque is clear enough, and only the astonishing ineptitude of Victorian criticism could have missed it. In the age when

Shakespeare's psychological insight was so extravagantly praised, it was common for critics to adopt a somewhat superior attitude to his verse, disapproving its conceited complexity, condemning it for not achieving what Shakespeare never intended, and only detaching for indiscriminate praise the "great passages" or "beauties" which were remorselessly anthologized. Subtler suggestions of "feeling" and "tone" we might expect to have been ignored, but this *Romeo and Juliet* passage is anything but subtle. Its blatancy is necessary to overcome the audience's natural tendency to join the Capulets in their mourning. And the audience must not do this, because their tears are to be reserved for the last scene. Surely it is more ironic, more dramatic, and more Shakespearean, to have first a burlesque mourning scene, breaking the tension and carrying the false assurance of a happy issue; and then to follow it by real mourning, when the star-crossed lovers have finally yielded to their destiny! The audience knows, it must be remembered, that Juliet is alive; and the audience has recently had cause to feel annoyed with the whole household of Capulet over the Paris marriage. They are therefore ready enough when prompted, to laugh at the gulling of these hardhearted elders, especially the old Nurse, whose lamentations, most clamorous and most ridiculous of them all, contrast so remarkably with the worldly wisdom of her traitorous advice not long before:

> Beshrew my very heart,
> I think you are happy in this second match,
> For it excels your first.
>
> (III. v. 223)

The scene, then, is differentiated into burlesque by the quality of the verse, and it ends in open comedy with Peter and the musicians. Yet even here we have more

than comic interlude.   The talk of funerals and dirges is
not without premonitory effect, and laughter will be a
trifle uneasy.   Then again, in the inappropriate surroundings of a burlesque mourning scene, we have a couple of
lines which might well have come later from Romeo in
the tomb—serious verse, standing out strangely from the
burlesque and pointing forward to a time when lamentations shall arise in good earnest:

> Death lies on her like an untimely frost
> Upon the sweetest flower of all the field.

(IV. v. 28)

This sentence, among so much nonsense, underlines the
necessity for constant attention and complexity of response in the Shakespearean audience.

The mixture of comic and tragic in Shakespeare is too
obvious to require elucidation by modern instances, but
it is interesting to observe that Hollywood preserves this
aspect of the popular tradition.   Passages of pure farce,
stylized and nonnaturalistic, still occur in quite serious
drama; and devotees of the detective film (or the detective novel) will remember the impossibly comic and in-
effective policeman who may obtrude into scenes of violent death and sudden bereavement.   This sort of thing
is often censured by the film critics whose correct "high
seriousness" demands unity of tone.   Any survival, however, of unsophisticated technique in the slick world of
commercial entertainment at least suggests a hope that,
beneath the polished coating of *ersatz* art, genuine artistic
qualities may lurk, perhaps to emerge in better times.

The Hidden Meaning

Myths and tales of the folk always suggest depths of
meaning beyond the mere sequence of events which they
narrate.   A late myth, such as the Cupid and Psyche

story, being a product of conscious art, is capable of directly allegorical interpretation; but stories of slow traditional growth are less susceptible of intellectual management, though their suggestion of hidden meaning is the more mysteriously insistent. The folk even today seem to require an "interpretation," a "moral," or a "lesson," before they are satisfied that a work of art has value; and this may account for the success of propaganda literature from Dickens to the "proletarian" novel of the moment. It is the critic, with ideas of "pure art," who resents this sort of thing; the earnest public likes its sugared pill better than those frivolous comfits whose sole justification is their flavor. In fact, one modern problem is the number of worthless literary sweets deceptively rolled into the shape of wholesome pills; the spate, for example, of "fictionized" biography, by which the public is persuaded to indulge itself under a counterfeit suggestion of learning. For the public likes to learn, but dislikes the drudgery involved in learning, and so falls an easy prey to literary vultures in owls' clothing.

This inveterate desire for pleasant instruction has not deserted the movie public; even the most lurid melodramas of the period before Hays Office censorship "only went to show that a girl must be careful," or to demonstrate the evils of strong drink or drugs. Nowadays Hollywood is perhaps more usefully employed in warning the American public against the innumerable varieties of "racketeering" which subsist among them. An Elizabethan audience probably listened with equal satisfaction to those passages of gnomic verse (printed in inverted commas in the early editions, to emphasize their moral content), in which correct moral attitudes were expressed towards the duties of parents and children, the dangers of wealth, and the necessity of order and subor-

dination in the commonwealth. But the Elizabethans
would surely go farther than these incidental passages in
their search for instruction; nor would they all be of the
mental caliber of Simon Forman, for whom the lesson
of *The Winter's Tale* was apparently that one should
"beware of trustinge feined beggars or fawninge fellouss,"
such as Autolycus![3] The Elizabethans had been brought
up in the "morality" tradition: they were used to seeing
virtues and vices directly impersonated upon the stage
and used, therefore, to the necessity of penetrating an
allegory in order to seize upon a play's full significance.
I have already stressed this point in discussing character,[4]
and it is also relevant to the general interpretation of an
Elizabethan play. It is hardly likely, when playwrights
and audience had for generations been used to plays with
a core of hidden meaning, that this interpretative element
should be suddenly abandoned, any more than that characters should change suddenly from pure allegory to bare
representation.

Moreover, the Elizabethan age was a theological age,
in which matters of profound doctrinal significance were
dealt with in the popular sermons from Paul's Cross,
and fought out in an endless stream of more or less scurrilous pamphlets. Every one was familiar with the complex methods of biblical interpretation;[5] and only the

[3] Quoted from Simon Forman's *Booke of Plaies*, in E. K. Chambers,
William Shakespeare. . . , I, 341.

[4] See Chapter V, p. 117.

[5] John Ashton, in *Humour, Wit, and Satire of the Seventeenth Century*
(London: Chatto & Windus, 1883), quotes (on pp. 411, 412) a comic
"Preachment on Malt" (taken from *Coffee House Jests Refined and En-
larged*, etc., The Fourth Edition . . . 1686), in which a preacher rebukes
some drunkards by a witty sermon. He begins by taking the letters M.
A. L. T., and explains: "These letters represent four interpretations, which
Divines commonly do use thus. M. Moral, A. Allegorical, L. Literal,
T. Tropological." Technicalities of interpretation must have been gen-
erally familiar, to find their way into the jestbooks.

Anabaptists, fathers of modern fundamentalism, desired that the literal meaning of the Scriptures should alone be accepted. Shakespeare's audience were accustomed to having the mystical significance of scriptural passages laid bare in their weekly sermons. And sermons were taken seriously in those days; by the elder members of a congregation they would be well criticized and discussed, while grammar-school boys of the period had even to memorize them for reproduction on Monday mornings without book![6] Now if the exotic and sensual *Song of Solomon* may be understood allegorically as the marriage of Christ and his Church (as traditionally and very properly it has been understood), then it is not unlikely that the exotic and sensual *Antony and Cleopatra* might also yield its hidden meaning to an audience simultaneously aware of the two levels of story and significance.

When Professor Wilson Knight, in *The Wheel of Fire*, began to interpret Shakespeare mystically, he was adopting a method congenial to the Elizabethan mind and to the tradition of popular art. Nineteenth-century critics were doubtful about the "moral," partly because "Art" was in process of declaring its superiority and indifference to morality, and partly because a moral so often appears as an awkward didactic appendage to a work already complete in itself. When I claim, however, that a play of Shakespeare has a significance beyond the mere story and characters in themselves, I do not suggest that this further significance is anywhere abstractly formulated; I should, in fact, resist the suggestion that single passages, however significantly placed, may be detached from their context and their thought ascribed directly to

[6] See L. C. Knights, "Education and the Drama in the Age of Shakespeare," *Criterion*, XI (July, 1932), 599-625.

Shakespeare. That error leads to the Swinburnian interpretation of *King Lear* and the backbreaking weight of
significance allotted to Gloucester's impatient outburst:
"As flies to wanton boys, are we to the gods" (IV. i.
38). Nor do I suggest that, in writing a play, Shakespeare was moved to inculcate some favorite lesson into
his audience. Apart from the last plays, where the dramatic technique implies something of a didactic purpose, I imagine Shakespeare as simply selecting a story he
thought would "work up well" and then writing it with
his conscious mind quite sufficiently occupied by the more
technical problems involved. But in order to write poetry,
his mind would be flung open to the widest and deepest
possible range of unconscious suggestion. And Shakespeare's was a mind that thought in image, so that metaphor packs into metaphor, producing the most surprising
collocations of apparently diverse phenomena; he thought
of time, and death, and eternity, in terms of a candle, a
shadow and an actor. Is it not likely that the large and
composite image of the story as a whole would serve him
as a metaphor or symbol for his attitudes to certain aspects of experience? The difficulty is for a modern,
dichotomized mind to comprehend the organic functioning of minds free from our own pathological division.
We think in abstract terms or, rejecting abstract thought as
illusory, plunge into the undifferentiated medley of sensory experience. But Shakespeare's sensory experience
was selectively adjusted to his intellectual functioning;
he took in so much of his image as was needed for thought
and used it as the implement of thinking. Light signified
life:

> Put out the light, and then put out the light;
>> (*Othello*, V. ii. 7)

> Out, out, brief candle.
>> (*Macbeth*, V. v. 23)

Shakespeare does not think of a great many other qualities and associations of the candle: its color, texture, smell as it burns, and so on, but only of the main *functional* qualities by which it may become symbolical of human life: its properties of light and heat, the way it burns out or is readily extinguished. Attention is directed by the intellect to some properties rather than others, and this selective sense experience is then utilized by the intellect in its approach to general problems. This is the organic mind, in which intellect and sense are united in one compound experiencing whole. I do not suggest, then, that a Shakespearean play is strictly allegorical, i.e., that it has been deliberately framed so that characters and actions have point to point correspondence with abstract qualities. Allegory, in the *Faerie Queene* sense, is often unsatisfactory anyhow; one either forgets the allegory to enjoy the story or ceases to be enthralled by the story in order to understand the allegory. But in Shakespeare, experience of the whole poetic drama is necessary to apprehend its significance, for the significance is made clear, not by abstract correspondence, but by the suggestion of the organic poetic structure. After experiencing the play, it is possible to achieve an abstract statement of its significance; nevertheless, the importance of the play does not lie in this abstraction, but in its embodiment in verse. The critic's task of abstraction is not the isolating of a playwright's "message," but a purely clinical analysis, only to be justified by the fuller response to the play as a whole, which should follow a close and leisured examination of its constituent parts.[7]

Antony and Cleopatra has been treated the least kindly of Shakespeare's great tragedies, with the possible

[7] Cf. Dr. Tillyard's "great commonplaces" (*Poetry Direct and Oblique*, pp. 22 f.).

exceptions of *Coriolanus* and *Timon of Athens*. The general outcry has been against its loose construction; Dr. Johnson, admitting the play's "variety," thought that the events were "produced without any art of connection or care of disposition."[8] Professor Schücking also deplores "a decided falling off" in the handling of the plot. He instances the scene on Pompey's galley, where the drinking song (he believes) "completely *isolates the scene*, detaching it from the context of the whole in a manner which is unequalled even in Shakespeare."[9] These charges, both general and particular, have been adequately rebutted in Mr. Granville-Barker's *Prefaces*,[10] where the tight and balanced construction is closely analyzed and the blame transferred from Shakespeare to those editors who, thinking in terms of localized scenes, produced an incredible number of them out of Shakespeare's properly indivisible text. The play is now seen to be a careful pattern of interwoven and contrasting episodes, all duly subordinate to the main design: the presentation of Antony and Cleopatra in the broad context of the Roman Empire.

A more serious problem is presented to the critics by apparent inconsistencies in psychology and a general failure to adhere to Aristotelian precepts. Even the revolutionary critics are troubled. Professor Schücking[11] feels a sharp discontinuity in the presentation of Cleopatra, between the royal courtesan of the earlier scenes and the tragic queen who in the end chooses death rather than to be the victim of a Roman triumph. Professor Stoll[12]

[8] See *Johnson on Shakespeare*, ed. Walter Raleigh (New York: Henry Frowde, 1908), p. 180.

[9] *Op. cit.*, p. 135. Professor Schücking's italics.

[10] *Op. cit.*, p. 121. In this chapter I have derived much valuable help from Mr. Granville-Barker's Preface, though my conclusions are very different from his.

[11] *Op. cit.*, pp. 119 f.   [12] *Op. cit.*, pp. 146-147.

finds the characters nobler than their deeds or their love "greater than their natures," and ascribes this, somewhat vaguely, to poetic and dramatic factors; whilst Mr. Granville-Barker[13] suggests that we are concerned with great action rather than psychology. Professor Stoll and Mr. Granville-Barker are thus in direct contradiction, one finding greatness in character rather than action, the other in action rather than character. None of these modern critics supplies an answer to their predecessors' problem; indeed, they share the traditional attitudes, and their attempt to isolate character and action is a precarious and inadequate solution. It remains true that, regarding the play psychologically, one cannot reconcile the vicious, the vulgar, and the commonplace in Antony and Cleopatra with the sublimity with which they are invested, especially as they face defeat and death. With a naturalistic approach to character, one might well regard Antony as a licentious old ruffian whose political and military talents are forfeited through lust; and Cleopatra as the Egyptian harlot, shameless, selfish, cowardly, and sex-obsessed. Their transformation in the end would then appear psychologically inconsistent, an unworthy dramatic trick to dodge the moral issue—implying a sort of conversion without repentance, or perhaps the glorification of splendid vice.

In any event, it is quite clear that we are not intended to think of Antony and Cleopatra as a lecher and a strumpet—or only in a strictly qualified sense. To do justice to Shakespeare, we must radically alter our critical approach, and begin—and end—with the poetry itself. What everybody has noticed in the verse of *Antony and Cleopatra* is its Brobdingnagian imagery; objects of tremendous size and power are constantly utilized to illustrate

[13] *Op. cit.*, pp. 111-112.

some quality of character or situation. The employment
of such imagery is not limited to one or two personages
in the play, but is characteristic of them all. There is,
in fact, no attempt to differentiate characters by the
verse they speak, except to some extent with Octavius
Caesar, whose verse is normally dull and flat and impersonal, or else staccato as he issues orders. But when he
speaks of Antony, or Cleopatra, or the Empire, his verse
too takes on the grandeur and dignity met with in the
others; for example, his description of Antony's military
asceticism:

> . . . on the Alps
> It is reported thou didst eat strange flesh,
> Which some did die to look on;
>
> (I. iv. 66)

and his speech on Antony's death is in the same high
strain. This pervading suggestion of size and strength
and importance conveys the imperial theme[14] and the
dignity of the persons involved. But it is more precisely
informative than this. In the first scene, for example,
the Romans watch in disgust as Antony, Cleopatra, and
their Egyptian train pass by. Philo, thinking of the old
Antony, remembers

> . . . those his goodly eyes
> That o'er the files and musters of the war
> Have glow'd like plated Mars. . . .
>
> (I. i. 2)

Antony has since become false to his position in the Empire:

> Take but good note, and you shall see in him
> The triple pillar of the world transform'd
> Into a strumpet's fool.
>
> (I. i. 11)

[14] *The Imperial Theme* is the title of a book by Professor Wilson
Knight, which, however, I have not consulted.

And then we hear Antony and Cleopatra:

Ant.: There's beggary in the love that can be reckon'd.
Cleo.: I'll set a bourn how far to be beloved.
Ant.: Then must thou needs find out new heaven, new earth.

(I. i. 15)

The lovers speak of their love in the same large way in which Philo speaks of Antony the general or Antony the triumvir. If he is "the triple pillar of the world," their love is even greater, for this world cannot contain it; the the new heaven and new earth of apocalyptic vision are alone adequate to circumscribe it. This speech in the first minute of the play looks forward to the "husband, I come" (V. ii. 290) of Cleopatra in her triumphant death —an instance of the close unity of Shakespeare's poetic conception. What I must immediately note, however, is the application, here and throughout the play, of the same colossal imagery—the world, the heavenly bodies, the gods, etc.—to the theme of empire and the theme of love. It is a deliberate equation, for these themes are conjoined too frequently for accident. Even Scarus, after the sea fight, exclaims:

> The greater cantle of the world is lost
> With very ignorance; we have kiss'd away
> Kingdoms and provinces—

(III. x. 6)

"kiss'd" as the verb; "kingdoms and provinces," the object of the verb: in this way, by purely literary means, we are compelled to feel Cleopatra's love as quite commensurable with the honors of war and statecraft against which it must be weighed. The lovers' ceremoniousness with one another—always "my queen" and "my lord"— strengthens the dignity of their love. There is no disguising its sensuality: "The beds i' the east are soft," says Antony (II. vi. 51); and Cleopatra can "take no pleasure in aught an eunuch has" (I. v. 9); but it is expressed in the poetry only. There is no attempt to show Cleopatra's sensual nature upon the stage—out of regard for the boy actor, says Mr. Granville-Barker.[15] How would the old Hollywood have rejoiced in Egyptian orgies, and a seminude Cleopatra strutting with the "sword Philippan" (II. v. 23) about an impossible palace bedroom! Such events in Shakespeare are off-stage, and, as revealed in the verse, can be delicately attuned to a tone of loving reminiscence. When Cleopatra does appear with her lover, it is her wit we admire and her changing moods which claim our attention. She is no stage "vamp," but her sensual qualities have been translated into the medium of words. It is not primarily to spare the boy actor's blushes or to avoid his incompetent rendering of female passion that Shakespeare adopts this method; for any degree of naturalism would have nullified the suggestion of the verse, and we should be back in good earnest with the problem of the naturalistic critic unsolved. But the poetic building-up process is continuous. Even the lovers' oaths bring the theme of world empire into the context of passionate love:

> Let Rome in Tiber melt, and the wide arch
> Of the ranged empire fall!
>
> (I. i. 33)

> Melt Egypt into Nile!
>
> (II. v. 78)

> Sink Rome, and their tongues rot
> That speak against us!
>
> (III. vii. 16)

While the two themes of love and empire are thus paralleled in power and grandeur, they are at the same time

[15] *Op. cit.*, p. 204.

sharply contrasted as conflicting alternatives presented
to Antony's choice. The contrast is geographically expressed, as between East and West, or Egypt and Rome.
"Cleopatra" and "Egypt" are almost synonymous: as
"Egypt" (III. xi. 51) she is upbraided for her desertion,
and she is addressed as "Egypt" in passionate reconciliation later: "I am dying, Egypt, dying. . ." (IV. xv. 18).
Octavius Caesar stands for the Roman qualities, as Cleopatra does for the Egyptian. Octavia is the translation
of Rome into woman; on the level of character as well
as plot, she is a projection of the theme of empire into
the theme of love: "Octavia is of a holy, cold, and still
conversation" (II. vi. 130). In stagecraft also, the contrast between Egypt and Rome is insisted upon, as Mr.
Granville-Barker has shown.[16] It is evident in the very
first scene, when the Roman soldiers watch grimly as
Antony and Cleopatra move across the stage with their
Egyptian train. Later, Antony has just agreed to marry
Octavia when, in Enobarbus' great speech, we are given
the poetic essence of what Egypt and Cleopatra stand
for:

> The barge she sat in, like a burnish'd throne,
> Burn'd on the water—
>
> (II. ii. 196)

it is more vividly Egyptian than any pageant furnished
out of properties. Again, in the next scene, Antony
promises fidelity to Octavia:

> I have not kept my square; but that to come
> Shall all be done by the rule;
>
> (II. iii. 6)

and at once *Enter* Soothsayer, whom we have last seen
in Egypt. The scene ends with Antony again under the
Egyptian spell:

[16] *Ibid.*, pp. 117 f.

> I will to Egypt:
> And though I make this marriage for my peace,
> I' the east my pleasure lies.
>
> (II. iii. 38)

Even adjectively the contrast is preserved. Cleopatra jeers:

> He was disposed to mirth; but on the sudden
> A Roman thought hath struck him;
>
> (I. ii. 86)

and Enobarbus: "He will to his Egyptian dish again" (II. vi. 134). Egypt and its attractions are insisted on throughout the play, and not least in the Roman scenes where they are intruded piquantly—or even farcically with Lepidus' drunken inquiries concerning "your crocodile" (II. vii. 46). Act III, scene vi, is interesting for its presentation of Rome in contrast. We hear first of the activities of Antony, and an impressive list is given of kings who have assembled to his standard:

> Bocchus, the king of Libya; Archelaus,
> Of Cappadocia; Philadelphos, king
> Of Paphlagonia; the Thracian king, Adallas;
> King Malchus of Arabia; King of Pont;
> Herod of Jewry; Mithridates, king
> Of Comagene; Polemon and Amyntas,
> The kings of Mede and Lycaonia,
> With a more larger list of sceptres.
>
> (III. vi. 69)

Caesar, however, is undismayed:

> But let determined things to destiny
> Hold unbewail'd their way,
>
> (III. vi. 84)

he says, enunciating the Stoic, Roman philosophy; and the name of Rome rings out once and again with an assurance of stability and security:

>   Let Rome be thus
>   Inform'd. . . ;
>
>   (III. vi. 19)
>
>   . . . but you are come
>   A market-maid to Rome;
>
>   (III. vi. 50)
>
> Welcome to Rome;
>
>   (III. vi. 85)
>
> Each heart in Rome does love and pity you—
>
>   (III. vi. 92)

as Octavia, deserted by Antony for Egypt, returns to her brother and her natural Rome-ward allegiance.

Egypt and Rome are thus opposed throughout the play; they represent contradictory schemes of value, contradictory attitudes to, and interpretations of, the universe. It is difficult to isolate these opposed systems in a brief space without appearing to dogmatize; and the reader must understand that a great many supporting quotations have been omitted in order to reduce the argument into a reasonable compass. The whole play should be read with the opposition of Egyptian and Roman values in mind. First, then, Egypt and Rome stand respectively for love and duty, or for pleasure and duty, or even love-pleasure and duty. Supporting quotations are hardly necessary here: Cleopatra embodies the love-pleasure principle, of which the "Roman thought" (I. ii. 87), the call to duty, is the negation. Closely related to this is the opposition of indulgence and restraint: in Egypt "Epicurean cooks" (II. i. 24) provided breakfasts as horrifying to Mecaenas as to the modern mind. Caesar is not at home in carousals:

>   . . . our graver business
>   Frowns at this levity,
>
>   (II. vii. 127)

he says. Antony's men must drink deep before the battle:

> . . . to-night I'll force
> The wine peep through their scars—
>
> (III. xiii. 190)

but Caesar allows a feast after due consideration of supplies:

> And feast the army; we have store to do't,
> And they have earn'd the waste.
>
> (IV. i. 15)

"Waste" is a significant word here, and the contrast is forced home by wedging this brief scene in Caesar's camp between two larger scenes with the forces of Antony.

More generally—and more philosophically—we have in the contrast between Egypt and Rome, the old opposition with which Shakespeare was concerned in the comedies and in *Troilus and Cressida*, between "intuition" and "reason"; on the one hand the final authority of the spontaneous affections, on the other the authority of worldly wisdom or practical common sense (Caesar is very like Ulysses in general outline). Antony had made, says Enobarbus,

> . . . his will
> Lord of his reason.
>
> (III. xiii. 3)

He clings to Cleopatra against all sober judgment (III. xiii); he is familiar and a little sentimental with his faithful followers (IV. ii), and heaps coals of fire upon Enobarbus (IV. v-vi); he is prepared to meet Caesar in single combat (III. xiii. 25). Caesar is cold and calculating; for reasons of state he will give up his apparently beloved sister to the lecherous old Antony, and in full and disapproving knowledge of Antony's mode of life:

> Let us grant, it is not
> Amiss to tumble on the bed of Ptolemy;
> To give a kingdom for a mirth; to sit
> And keep the turn of tippling with a slave;
> To reel the streets at noon, and stand the buffet
> With knaves that smell of sweat.
>
> (I. iv. 16)

He has a low opinion of the people:

> This common body,
> Like to a vagabond flag upon the stream,
> Goes to and back, lackeying the varying tide,
> To rot itself with motion.[17]
>
> (I. iv. 44)

Caesar would never be betrayed into Antony's abandonment of the solid benefits of the triumvirate. He will not be tempted into bravado by Antony's challenge:

> . . . let the old ruffian know
> I have many other ways to die; meantime
> Laugh at his challenge.
>
> (IV. i. 4)

Faced with the dead Cleopatra, he is either moved for a moment or speaks out of character:

> . . . she looks like sleep,
> As she would catch another Antony
> In her strong toil of grace;
>
> (V. ii. 349)

but he has just become interested medically:

> If they had swallow'd poison, 'twould appear
> By external swelling;
>
> (V. ii. 348)

[17] It is interesting to note how "vagabond," "lackeying," "varying," build up the uncertain rhythm; also how image and object interfuse. "Vagabond" and "lackeying" apply metaphorically to the flag image and literally to the crowd of which the flag is an image; "varying" goes equally with "tide" and "crowd."

and it is this point that he dwells on:

> Most probable
> That so she died;
>
> (V. ii. 356)

for his last words are merely a ceremonious close to the play, with little significance for character.

Caesar incarnates the practical reason, or worldly wisdom, with which are closely linked the notions of restrictive morality and political order (Stoicism and the Roman law). Antony has a foot in both worlds; I have already contrasted him with Caesar, but there are also points of comparison. He is a Roman and has his share of Roman fortitude; he has mortified the flesh for military glory; and if Caesar will sacrifice his sister for political ends, Antony will sacrifice her, Cleopatra, and himself in the same cause, at least until the lure of Egypt proves too strong. Antony's position is central, for the choice between Egypt and Rome is for him to make. It is Cleopatra who stands opposite Caesar, incarnating "intuition," the life of the spontaneous affections, with which are linked the notions of expansive morality and aesthetic order (it is the positive affections which transcend her "baser life" (V. ii. 293); while the dignity of sense experience is vindicated poetically in Enobarbus' great description of the barge incident).

Justice is done to Rome, but the tendency is to depreciate the Roman values. There is a machinelike inevitability in Caesar, accompanied by a certain calculating meanness. When he speaks for himself, his verse is deflated:

> Let our best heads
> Know, that to-morrow the last of many battles
> We mean to fight: . . . .
>
> (IV. i. 10)

Imperial corruption subdues the note of Roman virtue. The banquet scene, with Menas whispering insidious suggestions into Pompey's ear, attains a political *reductio ad absurdum* when the drunken Lepidus is carried out: "A' bears the third part of the world, man" (II. vii. 96). The next scene, which should certainly follow at once, as Mr. Granville-Barker says,[18] and not be separated by an act division, shows the Roman soldier at work, efficient and triumphant, but suspicious:

> Who does i' the wars more than his captain can
> Becomes his captain's captain: and ambition,
> The soldier's virtue, rather makes choice of loss,
> Than gain which darkens him.
>
> (III. i. 21)

With Shakespeare, the new Renaissance virtue of ambition is usually treated as a vice; so in *Julius Caesar* Antony tries to clear Caesar's memory of the imputation. That ambition is the soldier's virtue implies Shakespeare's judgment upon the soldier (cf. Othello's "big wars, That make ambition virtue!" (III. iii. 349)). Cleopatra's is the final verdict:

> . . . 'tis paltry to be Caesar;
> Not being Fortune, he's but Fortune's knave,
> A minister of her will.
>
> (V. ii. 2)

The Egyptian qualities crystallized in Cleopatra are correspondingly raised in our esteem by subtle poetic means. The materials are not very promising. This is the Cleopatra who

> ...will wander through the streets and note
> The qualities of people,
>
> (I. i. 53)

[18] *Op. cit.*, pp. 121-122.

or "Hop forty paces through the public street" (II. ii.
234), or even play a practical joke with "a salt-fish on
his hook" (II. v. 17), and, as she recalls,

> . . .next morn,
> Ere the ninth hour, I drunk him to his bed;
> Then put my tires and mantles on him, whilst
> I wore his sword Philippan.
>
> (II. v. 20)

It is easy to remember her as that certain queen who, in
her "salad days" (I. v. 73), was carried "to Caesar in
a mattress" (II. vi. 71): a mixture of hoyden and strumpet, with a strong flavor of Nell Gwynne. But Shakespeare, taking boldly for thesis that "everything becomes"
her (I. i. 49), transmutes these qualities by poetic paradox. No wonder Cleopatra's character worries the psychologist; it is not so much a character as an extended
metaphysical conceit:

> I saw her once
> Hop forty paces through the public street;
> And having lost her breath, she spoke, and panted,
> That she did make *defect perfection,*
> And, *breathless,* power *breathe* forth.
>
> (II. ii. 233)

The conceit is brought out by the resemblance of form in
words of opposite meaning, the opposites in Cleopatra
being resolved as the word sounds are assimilated. Again:

> . . . other women cloy
> The appetites they feed: but she makes hungry
> Where most she satisfies: for vilest things
> Become themselves in her; that the holy priests
> Bless her when she is riggish.
>
> (II. ii. 241)

Here again is paradox, and the fusion of opposites; there is a benediction upon her sensuality. Similarly of the love of Antony and Cleopatra:

> Eternity was in our lips and eyes,
> Bliss in our brows' bent; none our parts so poor,
> But was a race of heaven.[19]

(I. iii. 35)

Their love being heavenly, Cleopatra is herself a goddess. Enobarbus' description has a ritual flavor; and in the barge Cleopatra was actually dressed as Venus:

> O'er-picturing that Venus where we see
> The fancy outwork nature—

(II. ii. 205)

a characteristic hyperbole, for it is claimed that she excels Apelles' picture, which itself excelled nature. She habitually dressed as a deity:

> . . . she
> In the habiliments of the goddess Isis
> That day appear'd; and oft before gave audience,
> As 'tis reported, so,

(III. vi. 16)

---

[19] As I have already spoken of metaphysical conceits in this connection, it is interesting to note the rhythm of the second line here with its careful pointing by alliteration. It resembles very closely certain passages in Donne's Satires, including the famous

> "On a huge hill,
> Cragged, and steep, Truth stands. . .,"

and, so far as I know, reappears only in Benlowes and Gerald Manley Hopkins before the present century. Commentators have been worried by "a race of heaven"; Malone's paraphrase "of heavenly origin" is preferable to Warburton's "smack or flavour of heaven." I should like to suggest, very tentatively, that we may have here a metaphorical use of the "race" derived from *radix:* cf. "a race or two of ginger" (*The Winter's Tale,* IV. iii. 50)—or at least a fusion of this meaning with that suggested by Malone. In any event the general meaning is clear and of far-reaching significance. The lovers' poorest or least honorable parts (presumably the sexual organs) were the root from which the "heavenly" experience of their love had grown—or (according to Malone's inter-

says Caesar, who seems shocked. She has the mystery of divinity: "She is cunning past man's thought" (I. ii. 150); her nod, like Jove's, will be obeyed:

> Cleopatra
> Hath nodded him to her;
>
> (III. vi. 65)

she has the same sort of immortality as Keats's nightingale, in virtue of her symbolic function:

> Age cannot wither her, nor custom stale
> Her infinite variety.
>
> (II. ii. 240)

Her age is insisted on, that we may know her beauty and attraction to be perennial: she remembers her "salad days" (I. v. 73) when old Julius Caesar was in Egypt, and she is unchanged in beauty when she meets his son. Yet she describes herself as being

> . . . with Phoebus' amorous pinches black,
> And wrinkled deep in time.
>
> (I. v. 28)

This is perhaps the most significant phrase applied to Cleopatra. In blunt prose she is described as being sunburnt, old, and wrinkled. Taken literally, this would contradict all descriptions of her beauty: wrinkles were no more admired in Shakespeare's day than now; and sunburn, strangely enough, was regarded as a serious blemish:

> The Grecian dames are sunburnt and not worth
> The splinter of a lance.
>
> (*Troilus and Cressida*, I. iii. 282)

---

pretation) had proved themselves of heavenly origin, in the physical expression of their love. Both interpretations associate sensual love with religious experience and doctrine—an association which is continued throughout the play.

In Cleopatra's remarkable conceit, however, the common attributes of age and ugliness are taken as the material of immortal beauty. The passage is fully intelligible only if symbolically interpreted—if we allow the poetry to do its work. For poetically the "deep in time" gives her an infinite age: it does not suggest an old woman, but an immortal; and "Phoebus' amorous pinches" thus become more than a metonymy for sunburn—she is an immortal lover of the sungod, of Phoebus-Apollo, the god of poetry and song, the paragon of male beauty, and therefore a worthy mate for such as Cleopatra.

The choice which Antony has to make between Rome and Egypt is thus heavily weighted by Shakespeare on the Egyptian side. Antony is a lordly man, a natural Egyptian. In his Roman days he was prodigal of pains (as an ascetic differs from a careful man):

> . . . thou didst drink
> The stale of horses, and the gilded puddle
> Which beasts would cough at: thy palate then did deign
> The roughest berry on the rudest hedge;
> Yea, like the stag, when snow the pasture sheets,
> The barks of trees thou browsed'st; on the Alps
> It is reported thou didst eat strange flesh,
> Which some did die to look on.
>
> (I. iv. 61)

He was as magnificent in his Egyptian pleasures:

> . . . his delights
> Were dolphin-like.
>
> (V. ii. 88)

His generosity and bonhomie have been mentioned; it was his generosity that killed Enobarbus, a natural Egyptian with a deceptively Roman exterior. For Enobarbus tried time-serving—prudence, Caesar would have called it—and died in consequence, "by moonlight, of a broken heart."[20] Antony's love can measure up to Cleopatra:

> Fall not a tear, I say; one of them rates
> All that is won and lost—
>
> (III. xi. 69)

and the goddess immortalizes her mortal lover as he dies:

> O, wither'd is the garland of the war,
> The soldiers' pole is fall'n: young boys and girls
> Are level now with men; the odds is gone,
> And there is nothing left remarkable
> Beneath the visiting moon.
>
> (IV. xv. 64)

Antony chose Egypt, intuition, the life of the spontaneous affections, with its moral and aesthetic corollaries; of all which Cleopatra is the focus and symbol. Shakespeare does not satisfy the psychologists with his character of Cleopatra; but he does not attempt a character in the sense of Trollope, or George Eliot, or even Dickens. In Cleopatra he presents the mystery of woman, the mystery of sensuality, an exploration of the hidden energies of life, and a suggestion of its goal. Intuition or spontaneous feeling is opposed to practical wisdom, generosity to prudence, love to duty, the private affections to public service; and the former in each instance is preferred. Not that the Roman values are entirely repudiated: there is a case for Caesar, "Fortune's knave" (V. ii. 3) though he be. But the Egyptian values are affirmative; the Roman, negative or restrictive: the good life may be built upon the Egyptian, but not upon the Roman. It is a way of saying that the strong sinner may enter heaven before the prudential legislator. In *Antony and Cleopatra* the strong sinners meet their purgatory here. They do not desire or seek it; it is forced upon them from without—

[20] Granville-Barker, *op. cit.*, p. 226.

grace which visits them in the guise of defeat. Changes of character inexplicable by psychological determinism are readily explained if we perceive that Shakespeare is applying theological categories. Earthly defeat is the providential instrument of eternal triumph: it comes un-desired, but when it comes, is freely accepted, and so con-verted into a process of necessary cleansing. Antony's purgatory lies in military failure and a bungled suicide prompted by the false report of Cleopatra's death; Cleo-patra's, in surviving Antony and in the thought of a Roman triumph. In the end the better Roman qualities are needed to transmute the Egyptian into eternal validity. Antony dies,

> . . . a Roman by a Roman
> Valiantly vanquish'd;
>
> (IV. xv. 57)

and Cleopatra, too, would emulate the Roman virtue:

> Let's do it after the high Roman fashion,
> And make death proud to take us.
>
> (IV. xv. 87)

Shakespeare nowhere approves suicide outside the Roman plays, but in them he seems to accept it, along with the pantheon, as data. It would be wrong, then, to condemn these suicides as from a Christian point of view. Antony's and Cleopatra's view of the hereafter is hardly Christian, either, but their assurance is emphat-ically not pagan. Antony says:

> Where souls do couch on flowers, we'll hand in hand,
> And with our sprightly port make the ghosts gaze:
> Dido and her Aeneas shall want troops,
> And all the haunt be ours.
>
> (IV. xiv. 51)

This is not the shadow world of *Aeneid* VI. Cleopatra's death is more studied, as she symbolizes the affirmation of life. She, too, must go by the Roman way of negation:

> My desolation does begin to make
> A better life.
>
> (V. ii. 1)

In desolation she realizes her inalienable possessions, that she is above Fortune, whereas Caesar is "Fortune's knave." Deprived of earthly love, she is denuded also of her earthly glory, and sees herself

> No more, but e'en a woman, and commanded
> By such poor passion as the maid that milks
> And does the meanest chares.
>
> (IV. xv. 73)

She must realize her common humanity for her symbolic function to be of general validity. It is by deprivation and denial that she attains reaffirmation, on a higher plane, of her essential nature; so that she faces death and the hereafter in the fullest confidence, claiming Antony for the first time by the name of husband:

> . . . husband, I come:
> Now to that name my courage prove my title!
> I am fire and air; my other elements
> I give to baser life.
>
> (V. ii. 290)

Her death speeches are as fully sensual as any before: even

> The stroke of death is as a lover's pinch,
> Which hurts, and is desired;
>
> (V. ii. 298)

and she hastens to meet first her "curled Antony" (V. ii. 304) in heaven.

In *Lear*, Shakespeare struggled with the problem of evil; in *Macbeth*, with the problem of sin in a Christian universe. In *Antony and Cleopatra*, he returns to the old problem: what are the positive bases of the good life? He finds them in the affections, and the affections as rooted deep in the sensual nature. Of these Cleopatra is the symbol, sensual even in death; for, paradoxically, it is these Egyptian values which must survive death. Caesar, the worldly wise, is "ass unpolicied!" (V. ii. 310). However shocking to the Nordic man, this position is theologically orthodox. Caesar's sins are deeper-seated and more deliberate than the sins of Antony and Cleopatra, and his heart is entirely set on the passing world. There is significance in Cleopatra's greeting to Antony after his short-lived victory:

> Lord of lords!
> O infinite virtue, comest thou smiling from
> The world's great snare uncaught?
>
> (IV. viii. 16)

She is his good, and not his evil genius, rescuing him from an undue preoccupation with the world, which is a snare and a delusion (cf. the Psalmist's frequent use of the "snare" metaphor, e.g., Ps. 141: 10). Nevertheless, the Egyptian values need a Roman purgatory to fit them for survival; they are cleansed, through adversity, of the taint of selfishness. Antony kills himself in order to rejoin Cleopatra, whom he believes to be dead; Cleopatra looks forward in the same way to their future reunion. Purged of selfish fear, the element of self-giving inherent in the sensual nature is revealed in its eternal significance, while Caesar, on the other hand, has no such selfless hold upon eternity. This is one way of poetically stating the resurrection of the body:

> . . . she looks like sleep,
> As she would catch another Antony
> In her strong toil of grace.
>
> (V. ii. 349)

Perhaps here, as elsewhere,[21] the word "grace" may have a tinge of theological significance.

Verbal Ambiguity and Dramatic Irony

One of the most valuable pieces of modern Shakespearean criticism is Dr. L. C. Knights's little essay, *How Many Children Had Lady Macbeth?* Dr. Knights shows the futility of the sort of criticism that asks questions such as that which he chooses, rather misleadingly, for his title; and lays down a principle which I hope has been applied in this present work: that the plays of Shakespeare must be treated primarily as poetry. He says further:

It is a general principle in the work of Shakespeare and many of his contemporaries that when A is made to describe X, a minor character or event, the description is not merely immediately applicable to X, it helps to determine the way in which our whole response shall develop.[22]

Actually this is by no means limited to minor characters. In my treatment of the "character" of Cleopatra, for instance, I tried to show that we were not so much concerned with psychology, as with the concrete poetic expression of a complex interpretation of experience. But I should like to make a distinction which is not made by Dr. Knights. In the presentation of Cleopatra, character and symbol are inextricably interfused; and this is Shakespeare's normal way of writing. The statement

> Age cannot wither her, nor custom stale
> Her infinite variety
>
> (*Antony and Cleopatra*, II. ii. 240)

---

[21] Cf. Chapter V, p. 130, and *The Winter's Tale*, I. ii. 99.
[22] *How Many Children Had Lady Macbeth?*, p. 36.

can be interpreted directly of Cleopatra as a woman; and it is only the circumambient suggestion of immortality, with the heightened rhythm, which assists in building her up into the symbol of a way of life. In the mystical interpretation of Holy Scripture, however, a single passage may be taken as referring to two distinct facts or events: "The words 'a virgin shall conceive, and bear a son, and shall call his name Immanuel' (Isa. 7:14), originally referring to a maiden about to be married and a sign of a contemporary national deliverance of Judah from the kings of Syria and Israel, are explained to be significant of the birth of our Lord from a virgin (Matt. 1:22-23). The words of Hosea, 'I...called my son out of Egypt' (Hos. 11:1), originally a description of the Exodus, are applied to the sojourn of our Lord in Egypt when His Mother and St. Joseph fled there to escape from Herod (Matt. 2:15)."[23] The Elizabethan churchmen at their sermons, and the Puritans at their weeknight lectures, were familiar with this method of interpretation.[24] I have already argued that attention to double meaning in the Scriptures, together with the experience of dramatic allegory, must have suggested to both writer and audience the possibility of "hidden meaning" in the ordinary tragedy or comedy; although in the Shakespearean method such hidden meaning is normally a subconscious component of the total poetic experience. But there are also in Shakespeare certain passages of double meaning, where the two meanings are clearly separable, like the literal and mystical interpretations of Holy

[23] Dr. Darwell Stone, "The Mystical Interpretation of the Old Testament," in *A New Commentary on Holy Scripture*, ed. Gore, Gouge, and Guillaume, Part I, p. 689.

[24] It is the "tropological" interpretation, mentioned in the "Preachment on Malt" (see p. 139, n. 5), and is distinct from the "allegorical" interpretation, as of the *Song of Solomon*, considered above (p. 140).

Scripture, just quoted. The distinction is plain. The passage above, from *Antony and Cleopatra*, refers (a) directly to the character of Cleopatra and (b) indirectly to a general quasi-philosophical interpretation of the play; but the sort of passage I have in mind refers (a) directly to the immediate situation and (b) indirectly to a situation to develop later. As this is yet another call upon the multiconsciousness of the audience, it requires illustration.

It is, however, no new phenomenon to which I propose to draw attention; in its most obvious form it occurs widely in every type of drama, and is known to the critics as "dramatic irony." The essence of dramatic irony is that a character should speak (or act) truer than he knows. When Othello meets Desdemona on the shore of Cyprus, after their safe arrival through the tempest, he exclaims:

> If it were now to die,
> 'Twere now to be most happy.
>
> (II. i. 191)

What in its immediate context is a mere lover's hyperbole, the unfolding of events will convert into the literal truth. At the moment of its utterance, the audience should catch a hint of danger. There are many such hints in *Othello*. One which is more complex occurs just before the first temptation by Iago:

> Perdition catch my soul,
> But I do love thee! and when I love thee not,
> Chaos is come again,
>
> (III. iii. 90)

says Othello, parting from Desdemona. He sums up here in a casual phrase what he is himself far from suspecting, yet near to bringing about. When he loves her not, chaos indeed is the result; and perdition does catch his soul through the instrumentality of the demi-devil, Iago. So, at any rate, Othello himself would lead us to believe:

> Whip me, ye devils,
> From the possession of this heavenly sight!
> Blow me about in winds! roast me in sulphur!
> Wash me in steep-down gulfs of liquid fire!
>
> (V. ii. 277)

Dr. Leavis[25] says that, for the self-consciously heroic Othello, this is merely "an intolerably intensified form of the common 'I could kick myself' "; but Othello refers to the traditional torments of purgatory, and the passage is thus quite consistent with the diabolic imagery running through the play in close relation with the role of Iago.

In *Macbeth*, as Dr. Knights says, "everybody has noticed the . . . parallel betwen Macbeth and Cawdor":[26]

> He was a gentleman on whom I built
> An absolute trust.
>
> (I. iv. 13)

This is a clear case of dramatic irony, but Dr. Knights also points out the earlier parallel between Macbeth and Macdonwald:

> The multiplying villanies of nature
> Do swarm upon him;
>
> (I. ii. 11)

and shows very convincingly that the bleeding Sergeant's account of the broil looks forward to the horrors which Macbeth shall perform upon Scotland and its king. He quotes especially

[25] "Diabolic Intellect and the Noble Hero," *Scrutiny*, VI (Dec., 1937), 274.
[26] *Op. cit.*, p. 37.

So from that spring whence comfort seem'd to come
Discomfort swells.

(I. ii. 27)

I must add my own comment to this passage, as it perfectly illustrates the comparison I have already drawn with the tropological[27] interpretation of Scripture. It refers immediately to the "broil" then in progress: the flight of the kerns gives the "Norweyan" lord an opportunity to advance. But the passage also looks forward to the main theme of the play: comfort has come from the prowess of Macbeth on the present occasion, but discomfort will swell from the same source. The few words immediately following—curiously, they are not quoted by Dr. Knights—solemnly draw attention to this prophecy: ". . . Mark, king of Scotland, mark," says the Sergeant: a weighty reiteration hardly necessary to preserve the attention of the king—or of the audience—at such a juncture. Dr. Knights does not distinguish this "prophetic" method (which is also quite different from the overt prophecies used in the chronicle plays) from Shakespeare's normal fusion of story and interpretation; but this is clearly a fusion of two parts of the story. It is, I suppose, a sort of dramatic irony, though it may be distinguished from the more usual dramatic irony, dear to the dramatic critic. In the latter, a phrase dropped quite lightly gains overwhelming significance in the light of events; but here the phrase is equally significant in its immediate and in its remoter context.

I do not think that there are many instances of this sort of thing in Shakespeare, and I have no desire to exalt it into a "dramatic method"; there is no reason to believe that Shakespeare was conscious of what he was doing, when he transferred the method of prophetic exegesis to

[27] See p. 139, n. 5, and p. 164, n. 24.

his plays. But a contemporary audience might have noticed such things, perhaps, again, without being aware of noticing them, having two events simultaneously in mind as they would in reading the Bible. *Troilus and Cressida* provides one example so striking that I shall rely on it to dispel any doubts as to the actual existence of this "prophetic" element in Shakespeare. The lovers' first meeting is a queer scene, in which passion is overshadowed by doubt, and both doubt and passion are generalized on a plane of metaphysical uncertainty (this is what Professor Raleigh[28] regarded as the Romeo and Juliet business all over again!). Cressida urges Troilus to go, but, characteristically, her words contain a veiled suggestion that she would prefer him to stay:

Cres.: For this time will I take my leave, my lord.
Tro.: Your leave, sweet Cressid!
Pan.: Leave! an you take leave till to-morrow morning,—
Cres.: Pray you, content you.
Tro.:   What offends you, lady?
Cres.: Sir, mine own company.
Tro.:   You cannot shun
    Yourself.
Cres.:   Let me go and try:
    I have a kind of self resides with you;
    But an unkind self, that itself will leave,
    To be another's fool. I would be gone:
    Where is my wit? I know not what I speak.
                  (III. ii. 147)

My concern is with the last four lines. In relation to the immediate occasion of their being spoken, we may paraphrase thus: "I have a self which remains with you, even though I leave you (i.e., "my heart is still yours": the divided self is a common enough conceit, like the interchange of hearts); but this self, which remains with you,

[28] Cf. Walter Raleigh, *Shakespeare* ("English Men of Letters Series," London: Macmillan & Co., Ltd., 1907), p. 116.

is unkind to me, since it leaves me, so that it may be the
fool of somebody else" (or "be made a fool of by somebody else"). She then repeats her desire to be gone and,
affecting what a century later would be called "a pretty
confusion," admits that she does not know what she is saying—the blushing admission of a girl who has to explain
herself in an embarrassing situation. But now, in a further
paraphrase, let us apply the same speech to Cressida's
future behavior: "I have one self which remains with
you; but I have (also) an unkind self, which will leave
the self that is with you, in order to become the fool of
somebody else (i. e., Diomedes)." This prophetic interpretation is emphasized by the last line, which has now
a wholly different meaning: there is first a suggestion of
prophetic ecstasy ("Where is my wit?"); and then a
statement, now to be taken quite literally, that she does
not understand what she is saying. This last line, like the
"Mark, king of Scotland, mark," serves to draw the audience's attention to a speech of special significance, with
two distinct meanings of which they must be simultaneously aware.

CHAPTER VII

CERTAIN PROBLEMS

WE CAN NEVER be sufficiently grateful to Shakespearean scholars for providing us with a workable text. Certain aspects of Shakespearean scholarship, however, reveal the evil effects of substituting an imitation scientific method for the mature common sense and knowledge of theater, which are the best check upon extravagant theory and the best guide to a balanced evaluation of evidence. In this chapter I propose to deal with three famous *cruces* of Shakespearean scholarship, applying to the solution of each my principle of multiconsciousness.

Did Viola-Cesario Ever Sing?

The Shakespearean scholarship whose validity I doubt is tireless in discovering evidence of botching and revision, as if Shakespeare were constantly altering what he had written or calling in subordinates to assist him in composition. This strikes me as antecedently improbable. Shakespeare's whole manner suggests a quick, sure, and final writing; so does the evidence of Heminge and Condell, who surely were not so unscrupulous as to talk of having "scarce received from him a blot in his papers"[1] if they had never seen them. Shakespeare seems to me to be the sort of writer who would rather dash off a scene himself, than go to the bother of detailing its content to a hack; especially as he was a quick writer, hacks were slow, and hacks had to be paid. Nor can I persuade myself that Shakespeare would be bothered with revision; with his head full of *Macbeth* or *Antony and Cleo-*

---

[1] "To the Great Variety of Readers," prefixed to the First Folio.

patra he would hardly trouble himself to go back over *Twelfth Night* again: indeed, the *Twelfth Night* phase being past, return would be difficult, if not impossible. Again, from the theatrical point of view, neither time nor money would be spent on revising a script, unless it were strictly necessary for the introduction of new "business" or new effects. After the law about profanity, it would be necessary to run over *Twelfth Night,* substituting "Jove" for "God"—such a revision I can understand, though I cannot imagine Shakespeare as the reviser. I can also see that it might be necessary to transfer a song from one character to another; but if so, the alteration would be carried out with the minimum of trouble.

It was Fleay who first advanced the theory that *Twelfth Night* had suffered revision.[2] This was an extension of his belief that the song in Act II, scene iv, was originally sung by Viola-Cesario and afterwards given to Feste. The scene begins thus:

Duke: Give me some music. Now, good morrow, friends.
    Now, good Cesario, but that piece of song,
    That old and antique song we heard last night:
    Methought it did relieve my passion much,
    More than light airs and recollected terms
    Of these most brisk and giddy-paced times:
    Come, but one verse.
Cur.: He is not here, so please your lordship,
    that should sing it.
Duke: Who was it?
Cur.: Feste, the jester, my lord; a fool that the Lady Olivia's father took much delight in. He is about the house.
Duke: Seek him out, and play the tune the while.
                                    (II. iv. 1)

[2] This account I take from Professor Dover Wilson's treatment of "The Copy for *Twelfth Night*, 1623," in his edition of *Twelfth Night* for the *New Cambridge Shakespeare* (1930).

Professor Dover Wilson comments:

First, as Fleay notes, we have a request (in verse) that Cesario should sing the song, followed by Curio's strange answer (in prose) that the singer is not present and the, to my mind, still stranger or at least lamer, explanation (also in prose) of how Olivia's fool comes to be in Orsino's house. Furthermore, as Fleay adds, the Duke "afterwards points out the special character of the song (ll. 43-48) to Cesario, who had also heard it, and who had been just asked to sing it." Both adaptation and substitution are palpable.[3]

Mr. Richmond Noble, in *Shakespeare's Use of Song*[4] and in an essay, "Shakespeare's Songs and Stage," in the Shakespeare Association's production, *Shakespeare and the Theater*,[5] carries the argument for revision a stage farther by the introduction of technical considerations in respect of the song. I quote from his essay "Shakespeare's Songs and Stage":

One of the main motives of the comedy was Orsino's conservative attitude to music and his dislike of

"The [*sic*] light airs and recollected terms
Of these most brisk and giddy paced times,"

and his preference for simple unadorned sentimental melodies. Suitably, Viola was to have been presented to him as an eunuch who could sing and play music to him. But in the play as we now have it, she does neither of these things and it is therefore very plausible to infer that when the comedy was revived Shakespeare's company no longer possessed a leading boy who could sing and play the lute. Instead it is the domestic Minstrel Feste who sings. In the song which he sings before Orsino much of the point in the context is lost. The song Orsino calls for is plainsong, a product of unconscious art known as the folksong, whereas the one rendered is a highly finished art song, one of the songs of

---

[3] *Op. cit.*, pp. 91-92.
[4] London: Oxford University Press, 1923.
[5] See p. 4, n. 1.

the lutenists to whose productions Orsino was so much averse, and it does not accord with Orsino's description of it.[6]

This is a development of the argument first proposed in *Shakespeare's Use of Song.*

At this point Professor Dover Wilson, in the *New Cambridge Shakespeare* already quoted, takes over and amplifies the case for revision:

First of all, if (as seems indisputable) Feste has been foisted into II. iv and into Orsino's palace in order that he might sing "Come away, come away death" in place of the boy who played Viola, then the change, though a little clumsily effected in the scene in question, is cleverly led up to in I. v where at the Fool's first entrance he is accused of truancy, so that the audience may be prepared to find him impetticoating gratillities in other houses than Olivia's. Moreover, seeing that Feste's presence in the Duke's palace is referred to at III. i. 42-47,* and again at the opening of V. i when Orsino and the Fool encounter, it is clear that the substitution in II. iv was not just an isolated change in the cast for the sake of a single song, but involved changes affecting several scenes at least.[7]

Professor Dover Wilson goes on to argue that Feste differs from earlier clowns in being "a singing Fool, and something of a musician as well";[8] that it would appear that his part had been amplified in this direction, and reduced elsewhere "since though Maria announces that the Fool is to 'make a third' with Sir Toby and Sir Andrew as eavesdroppers from the box-tree in the letter-scene (II. iii. 189*), when we get to the scene itself we find his place unexpectedly taken by Fabian."[9] It is suggested that Feste has to be free in order to open the following scene with a performance on the tabor. "Is it not

---

[6] *Shakespeare and the Theatre*, pp. 129-130.
* References have been altered to correspond with the Globe edition.
[7] *Op. cit.*, p. 93.
[8] *Ibid.*   [9] *Ibid.*, p. 94.

a fair inference from all this," asks Professor Dover Wilson, "that the text of *Twelfth Night*, as we have it, has been revised, and revised primarily to give scope for a Clown with a voice?"[10]

For my own part, I do not think it is. The substitution of Feste for Viola-Cesario as the singer of "Come away, come away, death," is admittedly a better reason for revision than most, but I cannot believe that, if this substitution had to take place, Shakespeare would have done more than tinker with the one scene in which the song occurs. What we are asked to believe, however, is that the change should be "a little clumsily effected" in the scene itself, but yet "cleverly led up to in I. v" and supported later by references in Act III, scene i, and Act V, scene i —botched work at the important point, and very careful placing elsewhere of hints which only a scholar in his study would follow up. (There is a great difference between a hint at Feste's truancy and such hints at "inner meaning" as I have considered in previous chapters. An audience is alert to significances, but is easily blinded to flaws in plot construction, since the poetic drama demands attention to the verse and its meaning and distracts attention from the "detective story" level of plot consistency.)

Let us now consider the crucial scene. Professor Dover Wilson refers to "Curio's strange answer (in prose) that the singer is not present and the, to my mind, still stranger or at least lamer, explanation (also in prose) of how Olivia's fool comes to be in Orsino's house."[11] I cannot see *any* explanation, only a reference to Olivia's father and his delight in Feste. And why should not Feste be in the habit of picking up an honest penny at the Duke's? —it was not unusual for liveried ministrels to wander, so

[10] *Ibid.*   [11] *Ibid.*, pp. 91-92.

why not a musical clown? Why then does Curio speak
in prose, if this is not an insertion? But again, why speak
in prose if it *is* an insertion?—Shakespeare or anybody
about the theater could have turned a blank verse line
if required, as for example: "He is not here, so please
you, that should sing it," or again:

> Feste, my lord, a fool Olivia's sire
> Took much delight in. He's about the house.

Prose is used because prose is more effective. Orsino, the
burlesque Petrarchan lover, comes in calling for music;
naturally his sentiment requires blank verse. He does
not, be it noted, ask Cesario to sing, but asks Cesario for
a song heard the night before: "That old and antique
song we heard last night" (II. iv. 3). The "we" is
hardly a ceremonial plural, as the rest of the passage preserves the singular ("Methought," "my"); so that it
presumably means the Duke and Cesario. But if Cesario
had sung the song, the Duke would hardly refer to it as
"That . . . song we heard." The "Come, but one verse"
certainly looks as though Cesario is expected to sing; it
has the appearance of personal pleading. But, surely, if
Shakespeare was going to alter anything, he would have
altered these four words. Since, however, he has not
altered them, we must try to interpret them. The Duke,
in his sentimental love dream, comes in craving music;
we must remember that he is, like his passion, "high fan-
tastical" (I. i. 15). He has with him his page, Cesario,
who has become indispensable to him.[12] He remembers
a song of the previous evening, which he believes soothed
the passion he is so sedulously nursing, but naturally he
does not remember the singer. Such mundane considerations are left to Cesario. It is more in keeping with him

[12] See I. iv. 12 f.

to remember something of the character of the song, especially that it was "old and antique" (for lovers always look away from the cynical present to the romantic past), and to remember its soothing effect upon his lover's pain. And so he asks Cesario directly for the song, describes it —a little vaguely—and ends, a true melancholic lover, by pleading where he might have commanded: "Come, but one verse." Had he ordered the song to be sung, it would have jarred in unseemly contrast with his studied character of "plaintive lover." Curio's brusque prose breaks across the lover's dream, with a statement of hard fact: Orsino's passion may require the song, but the singer is not present. The use of prose is understandable enough. Again Fleay complains that the Duke afterwards points out to Cesario the nature of the song ("Mark it, Cesario, it is old and plain," etc. (II. iv. 44)), although Cesario had heard it the night before. But does Fleay imply that Shakespeare had inadvertently left in both references to the song's having been sung the previous night? That would indeed have been a remarkable oversight. Of course, actually, the Duke is just the man to expatiate feelingly but condescendingly to his page upon a matter known equally well to them both. It is beautifully in character.

And so we come to Mr. Richmond Noble. I need not pause long over the "very plausible" inference that Viola was at first "presented as an eunuch" to Orsino, but that a new version had to be written because the company no longer had a boy-actor who could struggle through a song. It seems most unlikely that no such boy would be forthcoming if there were a part for him. After all, Shakespeare's was an important company, used to command performances. As to the passage:

> I'll serve this duke:
> Thou shalt present me as an eunuch to him: etc.,
>
> (I. ii. 55)

it is curious that Shakespeare should overlook it, when he was so careful to scatter prodigal references to Feste's truancy up and down the play. But there is no need to think that Shakespeare has overlooked it: Viola's first idea is to serve Olivia:

> O that I served that lady
> And might not be delivered to the world;
>
> (I. ii. 41)

her second and more attractive idea is to serve the bachelor, Orsino; she will be presented as an eunuch, and entertain him with her music. Then, when we see her, we find that she is indeed serving Orsino, but as a young page of high birth—a very natural compromise. Or we may say that Shakespeare threw out the eunuch idea in Act I, scene ii, and forgot it by Act I, scene iv—which is not at all unlikely. In either event it is impossible to argue from this passage to Viola-Cesario as the singer of the song in Act II, scene iv.

Mr. Noble's special point is concerned with the song itself and Orsino's description of it; and it is to this point that my own theory of multiconsciousness most particularly applies. According to Mr. Noble:

The song Orsino calls for is plainsong, a product of unconscious art known as the folk-song, whereas the one rendered is a highly finished art song, one of the songs of the lutenists to whose productions Orsino was so much averse. . . .[13]

Admittedly, according to Orsino the song is "old and plain" (II. iv. 44), such as "The spinsters and the knitters in the sun. . . . Do use to chant" (II. iv. 45, 47).

[13] *Shakespeare and the Theatre*, pp. 129-130.

From "plain" to "plainsong" is rather a stretch—from the general epithet to the technical term; nor can I agree with another minor point of Mr. Noble's, that "Come away, come away, death," being a man's complaint, would hardly be sung by "spinsters";[14] but I admit the disparity between Orsino's description and the "modern" lutenist song. The song, however, for all its sophistication of manner, is not a song about sophisticated feeling; its attitude to love is not neo-Ovidian or Donne-ish or elaborately conceited Petrarchan. What it does is to present in a sophisticated manner the supposed simplicity of earlier days. The lover is dying of love, not cynically boisterous about it; he speaks of "sad cypress," his "shroud of white, stuck all with yew," and his "black coffin." It is not genuinely "old and plain," but it is romantically suggestive of antiquity and repudiates "these most brisk and giddy-paced times" (II. iv. 6), with the self-consciousness of Orsino himself. Surely this is a familiar situation to those conversant with the ways of music hall and musical comedy! "Come," says the old squire, "let us have one of the good old songs we used to sing in the days when I courted your mother by the old mill stream": the orchestra strikes up, and the juvenile lead in a dubious tenor breaks into one of this season's sentimental songs, in "swing-time," if about 1940, but appropriately peppered with references to the little thatched cottage, the roses round the door, probably the old mill stream itself, and whatever else might suggest the theme of old-fashioned simplicity. This—in a superior way, because Shakespeare lived in a musical age— is precisely what I believe to have happened in *Twelfth Night*, Act II, scene iv. It explains the apparent incon-

[14] *Shakespeare's Use of Song*, p. 84.

sistency between the song and Orsino's description of it, without the awkward necessity of a revision carried out with so surprising a combination of clumsiness and subtlety. The audience, always accommodating in such matters, would cheerfully accept the song as old *for the purposes of the story*, and at the same time enjoy it as a new lutenist "hit," on the level of musical entertainment, probably preferring it to "old-fashioned" plainsong. This is a mode of double consciousness quite elementary in comparison with much we have considered. And so there is no reason to believe that "Come away, come away, death" was not the original song in *Twelfth Night*, Act II, scene iv; and no reason to believe that it was not originally sung by Feste. As to the general question of revision, there remains the substitution of Fabian for Feste in the letter scene. Now Fabian is a useful character afterwards, much more appropriate than Feste in the matter of the duel, for instance; and if the need of some such character occurred to Shakespeare after writing Maria's speech in which the Clown is named as an appropriate third party for concealment in the box tree, but before the letter scene itself; then the substitution of Fabian for Feste would naturally follow. It would provide a slight breathing space for the Clown and build up the character of Fabian. As for Maria's suggestion, it was only a suggestion anyway; and one reason for the apparent "naturalness" of Shakespeare is that he does not bother to go back and correct such minor inconsequences. The revisionist argument avails itself, also, of certain possible references to contemporary affairs later than the first date at which the play was known to have been performed; but such references have to be very convincing to stand alone, and it has never been pretended that they are here more than slightly confirmatory of a case which, I hope, has now been shown to be entirely without foundation.

The Player's Speech and Hamlet as Dramatic Critic

The following paragraph begins Note F, "The Player's Speech in *Hamlet*," in A. C. Bradley's *Shakespearean Tragedy*:

There are two extreme views about this speech. According to one, Shakespeare quoted it from some play, or composed it for the occasion, simply and solely in order to ridicule, through it, the bombastic style of dramatists contemporary with himself or slightly older; just as he ridicules in 2 *Henry IV* Tamburlaine's rant about the kings who draw his chariot, or puts fragments of similar bombast into the mouth of Pistol. According to Coleridge, on the other hand, this idea is "below criticism." No sort of ridicule was intended. "The lines, as epic narrative, are superb." It is true that the language is "too poetical—the language of lyric vehemence and epic pomp, and not the drama"; but this is due to the fact that Shakespeare had to distinguish the style of the speech from that of his own dramatic dialogue.[15]

Professor Bradley agrees "in essentials" with Coleridge; but he feels that "with much that is fine there is intermingled a good deal that, in epic as in drama, must be called bombast." "But," he goes on, "I do not believe Shakespeare meant it for bombast."[16] The argument presents itself to Professor Bradley as a dilemma:

If the speech was meant to be ridiculous, it follows either that Hamlet in praising it spoke ironically, or that Shakespeare in making Hamlet praise it sincerely, himself wrote ironically. And both these consequences are almost incredible.[17]

Examining Hamlet's commendation of the speech, Bradley finds it "sincere in tone and manner,"[18] and he regards

[15] P. 413.   [16] P. 413.
[17] P. 414.   [18] P. 414.

Hamlet's subsequent behavior as confirming this view: since Hamlet twice snubs Polonius, first for objecting to the length of the speech and secondly for deploring its emotional excess, and later, when alone, "in contrasting this emotion with his own insensibility, he betrays no consciousness that there was anything unfitting in the speech that caused it."[19] So far Bradley has "chiefly followed Warburton";[20] he next proceeds on his own account, to compare Hamlet's later advice to the players and to find it consistent with his criticism of the Player's speech; he considers Hamlet's persistent objection to rant and decides that presumably "to Hamlet and Shakespeare"[21] Laertes' speech at the graveside of Ophelia is rant, but the Player's speech is not rant. There follows a list of passages from Shakespeare, which, in hyperbole and conceit, are said to be comparable to passages from the Player's speech; and the argument closes with the Player's speech apparently vindicated. It is impossible to quote the entire note, which runs to several pages, but Professor Bradley's work is generally accessible.

The case is well argued and its conclusion gains weight from the high authority of Coleridge's critical judgment. Nevertheless, I cannot persuade myself that a candid and competent reader can do other than regard the Player's speech as a delightfully amusing burlesque of the older type of "superior" Elizabethan tragedy in the Senecan tradition which *The Spanish Tragedy* first popularized. Critics, I suspect, have generally been so anxious to justify the critical acumen of Hamlet—the spoiled favorite among Shakespearean characters—that their first honest reactions to the passage have been ruthlessly repressed. If it is so, it is a grievous fault—the most grievous that a critic can commit.

[19] P. 414. [20] P. 414. [21] P. 415.

First as to Hamlet's criticism:

I heard thee speak me a speech once, but it was never acted; or, if it was, not above once; for the play, I remember, pleased not the million; 'twas caviare to the general: but it was—as I received it, and others, whose judgments in such matters cried in the top of mine—an excellent play, well digested in the scenes, set down with as much modesty as cunning. I remember, one said there were no sallets in the lines to make the matter savoury, nor no matter in the phrase that might indict the author of affectation; but called it an honest method, as wholesome as sweet, and by very much more handsome than fine.

(II. ii. 454)

Certainly Hamlet is serious enough; there is absolutely no indication that he intends irony. He is speaking soberly and carefully, though not very precisely in his criticism. After all, he merely says that the play was not popular, that it was "excellent," that the scenes were "well digested" (whatever that may mean—it may refer to action, plot, or verse), that it was free from salacity, and "very much more handsome than fine" (probably a metaphor from clothing). This is not criticism of a very high order; but there is only one phrase which makes one suspect Shakespeare of irony (though not Hamlet, in view of the context and what follows): there was "no matter in the phrase that might indict the author of affectation." Yet the speech begins:

The rugged Pyrrhus, he whose sable arms,
Black as his purpose, did the night resemble
When he lay couched in the ominous horse,
Hath now this dread and black complexion smear'd
With heraldry more dismal; head to foot
Now is he total gules;

(II. ii. 474)

an extended conceit in heraldry, which combines naïveté and pomposity in a remarkable degree. I cannot see that we may regard Hamlet's criticism as ironic, but I cannot see the least reason for regarding it as directly expressing Shakespeare's opinion. Contrast the colloquial energy of the advice to the players, with its rapid modulations in tone, its crowded and original metaphor, its general air of excited urgency:

Speak the speech, I pray you, as I pronounced it to you, trippingly on the tongue: but if you mouth it, as many of your players do, I had as lief the town-crier spoke my lines. Nor do not saw the air too much with your hand, thus, but use all gently; for in the very torrent, tempest, and, as I may say, the whirlwind of passion, you must acquire and beget a temperance that may give it smoothness. O, it offends me to the soul to hear a robustious periwig-pated fellow tear a passion to tatters, to very rags, to split the ears of the groundlings, who for the most part are capable of nothing but inexplicable dumb-shows and noise: I would have such a fellow whipped for o'erdoing Termagant; it out-herods Herod: pray you, avoid it.

(III. ii. 1)

I should say that in this speech and in the rest of Hamlet's advice to the players, we have Shakespeare's own views of acting, written with such energy that he half forgot Hamlet in writing them; but the criticism of the Player's speech is a horse of a very different color. It is correct and gentlemanly and quite adequate to impress the audience with Hamlet as a patron of the less erudite arts—a fairly typical young nobleman; but there is no reason to believe that Shakespeare had his heart in it; and one good reason to believe that he had not, for it is hard to maintain that the Player's speech is without affectation. Another more doubtful point is perhaps worth mentioning: the play is spoken of as "well digested in the scenes," and this suggests that it is a play written to the neoclassical formula which Shakespeare himself notoriously rejected, the act and scene division in Shakespeare being due in the main to misplaced editorial zeal. If this be so, then Hamlet is praising a type of dramatic composition in favor among the aristocratic dilettanti, but never successful on the popular stage; and it is difficult to believe that Shakespeare would wholeheartedly approve a mode of construction which he must himself have deliberately avoided. Hamlet, on the other hand, the aristocratic amateur, might well have shared Sidney's preference for the neoclassical. This would confirm my conclusion that the passage is meant to be taken as a serious expression of Hamlet's opinion, but not of Shakespeare's.

As to the speech itself, it is very clearly burlesque—not farcical, like the Pyramus and Thisbe play:

> Whereat, with blade, with bloody blameful blade,
> He bravely broach'd his boiling bloody breast;
>
> (*A Midsummer Night's Dream*, V. i. 147)

but a conscious attempt to bring out in a short space the distinctive features of the ranting tragedy. The rhythm has a fairly consistent thump, which suggests the sort of declamation Hamlet later deprecates. The language contains a high percentage of words of classical origin (a usage characteristic of the scholarly amateur): "the ominous horse" (II. ii. 476), "coagulate gore" (II. ii. 484), "Repugnant to command" (II. ii. 493); and stock epithets are constantly employed, inexact in meaning but vaguely emotive: "rugged Pyrrhus," "dread," "dismal," "horridly," "tyrannous and damned," "vile," "hellish," "antique," "fell," "hideous," "reverend Priam," "dreadful." This is a very representative collec-

tion of the hack poet's stock-in-trade, got together in remarkably few lines. The meaning, moreover, is diffused—
the direct contrary of Shakespeare's practice: Pyrrhus'
arms, his purpose, and the night are all black, and this is
conveyed with the maximum of repetition:

> The rugged Pyrrhus, he whose *sable* arms,
> *Black* as his purpose, did the *night* resemble
> When he lay couched in the ominous horse,
> Hath now this dread and *black* complexion smear'd. . . .
>
> (II. ii. 474)

Everything is overdone; "dread and black" *and* "dismal"; "total gules" ("gules" alone would be possible);
"Baked and impasted" (either alone might pass); "tyrannous and damned"; "wrath and fire." The blood is
overplentiful; Pyrrhus stands too long without movement; the descent of Fortune's wheel is too studied. And
there is the "mobled queen," a phrase which Hamlet
himself echoes, presumably in startled inquiry. This is
an interruption which Bradley does not notice. Surely
by this time the joke has become so good—the joint
joke of the speech and of Polonius—that Shakespeare
even allows Hamlet to come out of character for a moment and disapprove, so that Polonius may mistake him
and, trying to retrieve his position, say just the wrong
thing once again: "That's good; 'mobled queen' is good"
(II. ii. 526). Shakespeare, then, has compressed into
one brief speech the salient characteristics of the Senecan
tragedy: rant, Latinity, the stock emotive word; classical
reference; extended conceit; the classical simile "But as
we often see, against some storm," etc. (II. ii. 505);
exaggerated horror. Bradley's argument that individual
passages may be paralleled in various parts of Shakespeare is unconvincing. The "parallels" are, in point
of fact, not parallel: in *Richard II*, Richard refers to the

ground "which serves as paste and cover to our bones"
(III. ii. 154)—but is this at all "parallel" with "Baked
and impasted"? There is no parallel to "O'er-sized with
coagulate gore," but it is suggested that "the metaphor
by which in *III Henry VI*, V. ii. 37, Warwick's lips are
said to be 'glued' by 'cold congealed blood,' would strike
us as absurd if it were not now familiar."[22] There is
clearly all the difference in the world between the diction
of the two passages: the *Henry VI* passage is in everyday language, but the passage from the Player's speech
is, as usual, highflown and pseudo-poetic. The quotation
from *Othello* ("Whip me, ye devils," etc.)[23] is a description of purgatory, fairly literal, according to medieval "visions"; the passage from *Troilus and Cressida*[24]
is deliberately exaggerated as satire upon chivalry—and
so we might go on, examining each and finding a reason
for the use of such language, in the context from which
Bradley has extracted his quotations. But the whole point
about the Player's speech is that it crowds into so
short a time so much that requires apology. If Bradley
had been able to assemble strictly parallel passages by
drawing on the whole of Shakespeare (and the passages
are not genuinely parallel, as I have shown), this would
merely imply that Shakespeare occasionally ranted or
indulged in crude conceit; but the Player's speech is
solid rant and stiff with crude conceit throughout.

Can we, then, possibly imagine that Shakespeare
agreed with Hamlet, that he really believed the Player's
speech to be excellent dramatic verse? If he did, we are
to imagine him as spending a frustrated lifetime admir-
ing the high dramatic art of Kyd and his disciples, but
himself treading the lowly road which led to success at

[22] P. 418.
[23] P. 417. Cf. Chapter VI, p. 166.   [24] P. 417.

the Globe and turning out the world's best plays by sheer inadvertence. But Shakespeare was too clearly aware of the qualities of words for this to be thinkable: courtiers' jargon he found amusing from the time of Don Armado, and in *Hamlet* itself there is the burlesque treatment of Osric. Before *Hamlet* he had burlesqued *Cambises* through Falstaff, and the ranters generally in the doggerel which constitutes Pistol's normal speech; there were hints of such burlesque as far back as *A Midsummer Night's Dream*.

A general consideration of the players and of the Gonzago-play confirms my view of this earlier speech by the first Player. The company are traveling because they are down on their luck, unable to vie with the rising popularity of the child players, the "little eyases" (II. ii. 355): presumably they are rather out-of-date. It is noticeable that they have antiquated properties with them: the "bank of flowers" in the dumb show is the "mossy bank" so frequently used in Shakespeare's younger days. And in the play scene itself, Hamlet must have forgotten his previous approval when he calls out (rather like a privileged young blood on a shilling stool): "Begin, murderer; pox, leave thy damnable faces, and begin. Come: 'the croaking raven doth bellow for revenge'" (III. ii. 262). Significantly, he is telescoping with comic effect two lines of an old play, *The True Tragedie of Richard the Third*:

> The screeking raven sits croking for revenge,
> Whole herds of beasts come bellowing for revenge.[25]

His intention (and the intention of Shakespeare through him) is obviously to jeer at the old-fashioned ranting

[25] See note in Arden edition (ed. Dowden), p. 123; also Dover Wilson, *What Happens in Hamlet* (Cambridge University Press, 1935), p. 161.

type of play, of which the players' repertoire seems to consist. The Mousetrap itself is palpably bad in the main, though with a different kind of badness from the Player's speech: if parts of it are of Hamlet's composition, "some dozen or sixteen lines" (II. ii. 566), they do not reflect very favorably upon his literary judgment (though I doubt whether Shakespeare gave Hamlet's part-authorship a thought when he came to the writing of the play scene).

Almost everything, then, suggests that the Player's speech is burlesque (or at least not serious): the speech itself, the players' later performance, Hamlet's attitude to "the mobled queen," and his attitude in the play scene itself. It was, of course, necessary to write in a different style from the main play in order to distinguish the Player's speech and the play-within-the-play from the dialogue surrounding them. If an un-Shakespearean style had to be adopted, what more natural than to adopt an outmoded style—a difference in the time plane to reinforce the different plane of reality?   And what more natural to Shakespeare than to write it as burlesque, with a possible thrust at Alleyn and the company at the Fortune, which persisted in reviving the old favorites to a lower-class audience?   Indeed, could Shakespeare imitate such a style and not burlesque it?   We are left, then, with Bradley's dilemma; what he regarded as impossible, we are bound to accept as fact: namely, that Hamlet did commend the speech seriously, and yet the speech itself is burlesque. It is at this point that the concept of double consciousness enters as *deus ex machina*. It seemed to Bradley that if Shakespeare made Hamlet seriously like a piece which was palpably bad, then he must imply that Hamlet had bad taste. But this is to treat the play as if it were reality. I re-

ferred in my first chapter to a situation in one of
Mr. Harold Lloyd's comedies, which called for simultaneous attention on three planes: equilibristic performance, farce, and romantic adventure. The present
situation is simpler, requiring attention on only two
planes, and not quite at the same time. Watching Mr.
Harold Lloyd, the audience were thinking, "How
clever!" "How funny!" and "How dreadful!" all at
once, yet without confusion. In *Hamlet* they hear the
prince's commendation of a piece which is to be spoken,
and think "How clever! Just like my lord So-and-so,
who even now occupies a stool upon the stage." Then
Hamlet begins the speech of Aeneas, and there is time to
recognize the Alleyn rant, so that when the first Player
takes over, there is pure enjoyment of the burlesque;
and perhaps a realization that Shakespeare is "getting
at" a rival company. It is still easy, however, to switch
back to the Hamlet point of view, in order to side with
him against Polonius on the matters of length and emotion and, when the speech is over, to return permanently
to the story-level and so to a sympathetic hearing of the
soliloquy: "O, what a rogue and peasant slave am I!"
(II. ii. 576.) The impossible dilemma is the actual fact:
the Player's speech is taken by the double consciousness
of the audience as (a) serious for Hamlet, and (b) actually burlesque; such an attitude being easy and natural
where there is clear consciousness of the play as play.
The Bradleyan attitude, on the other hand, which was
not only Bradleyan but as old as Warburton, comes from
a false application of the categories of naturalistic dramatic illusion to a play where they are particularly out
of place.

Does the King See the Dumb Show?

Lastly, I come to the chief of Shakespearean *cruces,* a problem which has exercised the—to my mind, misguided—ingenuity of a number of Shakespearean scholars. "This," says Professor Dover Wilson, in *What Happens in Hamlet,*

This is the crux from which, as explained in Chapter I, the whole present inquiry set out, the crux to which Dr. Greg first directed the serious attention of critics and on which he himself erected a new and comprehensive theory of Hamlet.[26]

Curiously enough, it is also the crux from which my present inquiry set out, the problem which first caused me to ruminate upon the multiconsciousness of a popular unsophisticated theater audience. On reading Professor Dover Wilson's solution of the problem, I felt at once that the truth must be something much less involved than that—something quite simple, though perhaps obscure. Such, I think, is my theory of multiconsciousness. I can believe in any amount of complexity outside the conscious processes of the human mind: the universe is complex, the human body is complex, the human mind is even very much more complex, especially when taken, as it naturally is, in its social environment. But the conscious processes of the human mind are relatively simple; which is why, as the scientific movement evolved out of the Renaissance, it adopted the simplicity of the universe as its dogma, or ground of faith—not that the universe *is* simple, but that it *had to be* simple in order to be understood by scientific method. Here in the beginning of science are the beginnings of "wishful thinking." But the method of abstraction and simplification, which has led science into its practical successes, can never disclose

[26] Pp. 149-150.

the true nature of the universe, since only certain aspects of experience are amenable to such abstractive treatment, and there is nothing compulsive about conclusions based on abstraction from a small fraction of the evidence. Science is concerned only with those aspects of the universe which may be measured, or concerning which verifiable hypotheses may be projected. The arts, on the other hand, are concerned to interpret the whole of experience; and this is why it is a major disaster when the arts become unduly influenced by scientific method. The tendency then is towards a simplification of artistic composition (analogous to the "simplicity" of science), coupled with a respect for "fact"; and the result is naturalism, an attempt directly to imitate nature. There can, of course, be no true naturalism, only an approximation to it; but the mere attempt at naturalism is sufficient to rob an art-form of its capacity for subtle integration. Similarly, to criticize by scientific or "rational" methods is to fish with a net of such wide mesh that all but the coarsest fish get clean away. Criticism must take into account the subtle irrationality of unconscious mental processes and, at the same time, knowing human nature, remain skeptical in the face of apparent complexity on the conscious plane.

The problem of the dumb show is briefly as follows. The Gonzago-play in *Hamlet*—the "Mouse-trap" (III. ii. 247), which is to "catch the conscience of the king" (II. ii. 634)—is preceded by a dumb show which represents, in detailed pantomime, Claudius' murder of the late king by pouring poison into his ear. The play and the dumb show preceding it are performed before the king and his court. The king is apparently unmoved by the dumb show, but leaves in confusion when the poison episode is reached in the Gonzago-play itself. Why was he not thrown into consternation by the dumb show, in which the action is quite clear and unmistakable? Various solutions have been hazarded, most of which it would be idle to discuss. Dr. Greg, for example, arrived at the remarkable conclusion that, since the king watched the dumb show unmoved, he was not guilty of his brother's murder, and the Ghost's story was untrue. But liars on the stage are pretty clearly branded; had Shakespeare intended the Ghost as the villain of the piece, there would have been some one on the stage to tell us so. We must also be chary of accepting any interpretation of the mere events of a play, which entirely contradicts a traditional interpretation of three hundred years' standing. Dr. Greg has no more chance of general acceptance than Professor Wilson Knight, who shares his tenderness for the character of King Claudius.[27] I must also reject summarily the view that Hamlet deliberately applies a double test to Claudius, and that Claudius survives the first, in the dumb show, but succumbs to the second, in the play itself. There is no indication in the text that such is Hamlet's intention, but there is every indication to the contrary, as Professor Dover Wilson has shown.[28]

The most formidable theory is that of Professor Dover Wilson himself. He begins by showing that the dumb show is not there by inadvertence; it is not a relic of the old play, which Shakespeare has left in without realizing the difficulty it causes. Although so often omitted in modern productions, it performs a service quite necessary if the audience is unfamiliar with the story. For the dumb show, by representing the murder

[27] *The Wheel of Fire*, chap. iii, pp. 34 f., esp. p. 49: "Claudius is a good king, and the Ghost but a minor spirit."
[28] *What Happens in Hamlet*, pp. 151 f.

which they have heard the Ghost describe, indicates to the audience how Hamlet is about to test King Claudius, so that, sharing Hamlet's knowledge, they may watch for the moment of the king's self-betrayal. So far I am in complete agreement with Professor Dover Wilson. But now his theory becomes so ingenious as to be incredible. Shakespeare needed the dumb show, argues Professor Dover Wilson; but Hamlet did not! Hamlet had timed his effect for the play itself, after the preliminaries about second marriage; and the dumb show is an unexpected interpolation of the players. When it begins, Hamlet is fearful that his plot may fail, and his exclamation, "Marry, this is miching mallecho; it means mischief" (III. ii. 147), is an angry outburst against the players. Again, when the Prologue appears, Hamlet, taking him for a "presenter," expects that he will perform the presenter's usual office and explain the dumb show. The remark to Ophelia betrays his concern: "the players cannot keep counsel; they'll tell all" (III. ii. 151). The players do keep counsel, however, and the Prologue speaks his harmless posy. This second remark of Hamlet shows also that he had observed that the dumb show itself for some reason had not betrayed his intention—presumably the king had been looking away. This is underlined by Claudius' later inquiry: "Have you heard the argument? Is there no offence in't?" (III. ii. 242.) To quote again from *What Happens in Hamlet*:

The query, unconsciously repeating Ophelia's word, unheard by the questioner because spoken aside to Hamlet [i.e. "Belike this show imports the argument of the play" (III. ii. 149)], makes it certain that the king cannot have seen the dumb-show, which *is* the argument of the play, as every member of the audience is now aware.[29]

[29] P. 159.

The trouble with this theory is its crossword type of ingenuity. Could any one, on seeing the play, derive from those two sentences, "This is miching mallecho . . ." (III. ii. 147) and "The players cannot keep counsel . . ." (III. ii. 151), all, or even the essentials, of what Professor Dover Wilson sees in them? This is not, be it understood, listening to poetry so as to realize its full implications of thought and feeling; but listening to prose so as to deduce actions and motives not directly represented. The former mode of attention was, I believe, well understood among the Elizabethans, but the latter has only become usual with the dramatizing of novels of detection. I cannot believe that from those two sentences the audience could understand that the dumb show was none of Hamlet's devising, and that he was both angry and disturbed by it. The alliterative "miching mallecho. . .means mischief" is too much a part of the "antic manner" to be taken so seriously, and its first obvious meaning is a dark reference to the play's function as "Mouse-trap." Again "The players cannot keep counsel" has its obvious meaning: "it is a player's job to disclose things." If Hamlet had been suddenly angry at the players' blundering, he would hardly have been given expressions of anger which, delivered in a different tone, may be—and have been constantly—interpreted quite differently and yet appropriately to the context. I think it is fairly clear that Professor Dover Wilson's interpretation requires more "reading in" than any member of an audience is capable of spontaneously supplying. Had Shakespeare intended the dumb show to be taken as an unfortunate interpolation due to the players' excess of zeal, he would have taken steps that this should be quite clearly understood. Similarly with the behavior of Claudius. If Shakespeare had intended Claudius not to see the dumb show, he would have inserted something quite definite into the dialogue to inform the audience of the position. The Elizabethan drama relies fundamentally on words, not "business," and any special business is clearly indicated in the dialogue; it is not left to stage directions or the discretion of the actor. I do not know anywhere in Shakespeare where a matter of "business" so important to the plot is left without adequate direction in the dialogue itself. Yet all we have from Claudius is the query, "Have you heard the argument? Is there no offence in't?," as he becomes disturbed at the pointed reference to second marriages. The fact that he says "Have you *heard*. . .?" proves that he is not directly referring to the dumb show. Had Shakespeare wished to indicate here that Claudius had missed the dumb show, he would at least have worded the inquiry "Have you *seen* the argument?" There would then be real point in the comparison with Ophelia's "Belike this show imports the argument of the play." All that Claudius asks at this point is whether Hamlet is familiar with the plot. To say that Claudius must have known the argument if he had seen the dumb show is to beg a large question and to miss the resolution of the difficulty.

I suggest, then, that all the evidence leads us into an apparent dilemma: the dumb show reveals the plot of the Gonzago-play, yet Claudius sees the dumb show and remains unmoved—or at least remains in his place without making any audible comment. Professor Dover Wilson's case depends on a strained interpretation of every remark he seizes on—an interpretation different, in every instance, from the obvious meaning that the words would bear; his conclusion that Claudius is looking away rests on the slenderest positive argument. Indeed, the only cogent argument against the king's having seen the dumb show is the negative one from which the whole affair takes its rise; he cannot have seen it, because he displays no sign of having understood its significance. Professor Dover Wilson, having decided that Claudius has not seen the dumb show, goes on to indicate the conversation which absorbed him at the critical moment:

Here I need only register my belief that the King's conversation begins, not with Gertrude, but with Polonius, when, as Hamlet supports the love-distraught theory by throwing himself at Ophelia's feet, the old man exultantly exclaims "Oho! do you mark that?" (III. ii. 118); that its subject is Hamlet's behaviour to Ophelia and the standing dispute between King and Chief Councillor concerning the cause of his madness; and that the Queen is forced to join in, in order to hide her own confusion, by Hamlet's cruel sally: "for look you how cheerfully my mother looks, and my father died within's two hours" (III. ii. 132). It is conjecture, of course, but conjecture based upon the text, growing naturally out of the general dramatic situation, and withal— or so I venture to hold—the only possible way of playing the scene, if the previous lines of my argument are sound.[30]

Let the actors be the most subtle and intelligent in the world, how, without the use of dialogue and while the dumb show is naturally focusing the main attention, may they indicate that they are discussing whether Hamlet's madness originated in frustrated love or frustrated ambition? I submit that the feat is impossible and that Professor Dover Wilson, although he frequently refers to the practical question of production, is actually envisaging *Hamlet*, not as a play, but as a piece of history. To imagine a conversation of which not one word is recorded, may be a useful, if dangerous, exercise for the historian; it is outside the sphere of the dramatic critic. There is still, then, no positive evidence that the king did not see

[30] *What Happens in Hamlet*, p. 160.

the dumb show, and we are therefore bound to assume that he did see it, in common with the rest of the court. Yet, although it reproduced the murder he had committed, he gave no sign of alarm and uttered no revealing word. He sat firm until the same action was repeated with dialogue, and then he left the room in incontinent anger and alarm, at the point when the poisoning is again enacted.

In applying the principle of multiconsciousness, it is well to have recourse to modern instances. I have had frequent occasion to refer to the modern movie, music hall, or musical comedy, not because I regard such entertainment as necessarily excellent in itself, but because, in such an audience, it is still possible to unearth the relics of a natural and technically unsophisticated response. It is impossible to say anything directly about what went on in the minds of our Elizabethan audience; but we may be fairly sure that, despite differences of cultural environment, the basic unconscious attitudes to dramatic illusion, prevalent in the modern motion picture theater, are little different from those of an audience at Shakespeare's Globe. "Values" change more rapidly because notions of value are conscious before becoming unconscious and habitual. But the attitude to dramatic illusion is unconscious first, and only becomes conscious through critical analysis; so that naturalism is essentially a "high-brow" product, the fruit of reflection upon the unreasonableness of normal dramatic procedure. It is therefore necessary to ignore everything but "popular" entertainment in the search for audience reactions which may be valid for Elizabethan times. But if a modern movie audience will react spontaneously and unconsciously in a complex way, then, in a similar situation, it is not unreasonable to postulate a similar complexity of response on the part of an Elizabethan audience, since the change in cultural environment has militated against, and not in favor of, such spontaneity.

I should like to draw attention to an aspect of the "play-within-the-play" situation in the modern motion picture. We were inundated some time ago with films of stage life, in which elaborate variety shows formed a chief attraction. The story would usually have to do with the difficulties encountered by a company in producing a new show; the film would be punctuated by "shots" of particular scenes in rehearsal and would culminate in generous excerpts from the show, when it had finally achieved its opening night on Broadway. Now this variety show within the film was presented as if taking place on a theater stage; we might be shown first a shot of the theater, with its expectant audience, and then a shot of the opening "turn," with the footlights and orchestra pit still visible. But the Hollywood studio is naturally capable of staging a spectacle much more elaborate than any actual theater could contain: it is not limited by considerations of space; there is abundant time for changes of scenery and costumes, etc. And so the habit grew of establishing the suggestion of a theatrical performance by a shot of the theater and perhaps, as I said, an opening number, during which the orchestra pit was still visible; and then presenting a show of such elaboration that it would be quite impossible to fit it into the framework of a theater; but the theatrical atmosphere would be maintained by an occasional shot of an applauding audience or another glimpse of orchestra or wings. The convention has developed to such a degree that I have seen natural settings introduced into what purports to be a stage show. For example, in one film I remember, the suggestion of stage show was obtained in the usual way, by glimpses of audience, wings, and the stage itself; and the show (i.e., the show-within-the-film, which corresponds to the play-within-the-play) started with a scene in a winter sports hotel, apparently on a mountain top. This scene might well have been set up on an ordinary stage of reasonable dimensions: but, after a song-and-dance performance, "leading lady" and "juvenile lead" assumed skis, and we actually saw them speeding down snow-clad slopes and arriving at the mountain foot amid a crowd of enthusiastic spectators. The scene at the mountain foot was also quite capable of being mounted on an ordinary stage, and the atmosphere of stage performance was renewed for us by, I think, a glimpse of the applauding audience. Now this, I imagine, would be upsetting to the naturalistic critic. The movie audience are asked to believe that an elaborate ski-run may be performed on a stage within an actual theater; and we know that this is impossible. But, in point of fact, the audience are not dismayed; they accept the performance on two planes of consciousness at the same time: (a) as stage show, for the purpose of the story, and (b) directly as entertainment, which, if they paused to reflect, they would know could not be presented on a theater stage. Of course, in the main, they do not pause to reflect: they accept the show directly as entertainment, except when their attention is specifically directed to it as part of the story. In thinking of it as part of the story, they think of it as taking place on a stage; but in regarding it as entertainment, they do not think of it as taking place anywhere in particular. Perhaps my multi-consciousness may appear suspiciously like dullness: actually it is more like the acceptance of a mechanical contrivance without wanting to know how it works. In any event, it is a fact—and that is all I am anxious to establish.

To return to *Hamlet* and the dumb show: everyone has noticed that this is an unusual kind of dumb show. Usually a dumb show is fairly cryptic, a pantomime of allegorical figures, which provides a veiled hint at what the play itself is to be about. Each act of *Gorboduc* was preceded by such a performance, and, in the printed version, these are described and explained, as for example:

> *The Order of the Domme Shew before the First Act,*
> *and the Signification Thereof.*

First the musicke of violenze began to play, during which came vpon the stage sixe wilde men clothed in leaues; of whom the first bare in his necke a fagot of small stickes, which they all, both seuerally and together, assayed with all their strengthes to breake; but it could not be broken by them. At the length, one of them plucked out one of the stickes and brake it; and the rest plucking out all the other stickes one after an-other did easely breake them, the same being seuered, which, being con-ioyned, they had before attempted in vaine. After they had this done, they departed the stage, and the musicke ceased. Hereby was signified that a state knit in vnitie doth continue strong against all force, but being diuided is easely destroyed; as befell vpon Duke Gorboduc diuiding his land to his two sonnes, which he before held in monarchie, and vpon the discention of the brethren to whom it was diuided.[31]

This explanation would not be given on the stage, but the audience would have to interpret the dumb show, so far as they could, out of a general knowledge of symbolic expression. In *The Spanish Tragedy*[32] we have the following:

> *Enter a Dumb-Show*
> *Ghost:* Awake, Revenge; reveal this mystery.
> *Revenge:* Lo! the two first the nuptial torches bore
>   As brightly burning as the mid-day's sun;

[31] Adams (ed.), *op. cit.*, p. 505.
[32] I. Schick's edition (London: J. M. Dent & Sons, Ltd., 1898).

But after them doth Hymen hie as fast,
Clothed in sable and a saffron robe,
And blows them out, and quencheth them with blood,
As discontent that things continue so.
Ghost: Sufficeth me; thy meaning's understood,
And thanks to thee and those infernal powers,
That will not tolerate a lover's woe.—
Rest thee, for I will sit to see the rest.
Revenge: Then argue not, for thou hast thy request.

(III. xvi. 27)

Here also the dumb show is a parade of allegorical figures, who might not even be fully recognizable to the
audience. This time, however, there is a presenter, Revenge, to explain who they are and what they are doing,
so that the Ghost can interpret the "mystery" for himself. Yet even after the presenter's speech, the audience
might remain in partial ignorance, since they have not the
Ghost's intimate knowledge of what has happened before
the play opens; the presenter merely states the allegory
in words, but does not explain it. The audience would be
prepared for something to do with marriage and for a
deed of blood, but even with the presenter to help them,
they have no fuller information than this.

The dumb show in *Hamlet*, on the other hand, actually presents beforehand the action of the Gonzago-play,
only performed without words. This is not the normal
type of dumb show; to present the action beforehand like
this is to run the risk of boring an audience by repeating
it in the scene which follows. But, as has been well understood, Shakespeare does not use the dumb show for
the benefit of the stage audience (Claudius and his court)
but for the benefit of the actual audience, that they might
know Hamlet's purpose in the presentation of the Gonzago-play. The audience share Hamlet's knowledge of

the Ghost's speech and know that he wishes to trap Claudius into an admission of guilt; they know that the play
is to be a trap, but they do not know how until they see
the dumb show and realize that the Gonzago-play is to
reproduce the actual murder of Hamlet's father. And
yet Claudius sees it and remains in his place without a
word. Surely the explanation lies in the double consciousness of the audience. The stage show forming part of a
film story, is accepted in two ways, as I have shown: first,
in its direct relationship to the audience, as entertainment; and secondly, despite the impossibility of its production on a theater stage, it is accepted for the sake of
the story as an ordinary stage show, presented to the theater audience of which we are given an occasional
glimpse. In the same way, then, the dumb show in *Hamlet* is accepted by the (actual) audience in two ways: (a)
as a direct explanation to them about the nature of the
Gonzago-play and the need to watch the reactions of
King Claudius; and (b) as being, so far as Claudius and
the rest of the stage audience are concerned, a perfectly
normal dumb show—a symbolical hint which may or may
not give them an inkling as to the nature of the Gonzago-
play to follow. Moreover, Shakespeare has lightened any
strain upon credulity by omitting the usual presenter:
there is only a Prologue with a posy. The behavior of
Claudius is now quite understandable; he has seen the
dumb show, but he has only seen a symbolic reference to
murder. Perhaps he may be represented as a little uneasy, but no more than that—for murder is not an unusual dramatic theme. It is only when the dialogue of
the Gonzago-play forces home the parallel to his own ill
deed that he rises and hastens from the room in the first
confusing knowledge that his guilt has been discovered.
The dumb show he can watch in comparative equanimity;

for the audience know that, however it may be used for private communication between the author and themselves, a dumb show is, after all, only a dumb show, the darkest hint at what is to follow; and that there is, therefore, no occasion, as yet, for King Claudius to panic. He is not in their privileged position of intimacy with the author.

INDEX